Out of Control?

God's Sovereignty in an Uncertain World

Edited by Ali Hull

Authentic

10 09 08 07 06 05 04   7 6 5 4 3 2 1

First published in 2004 by Authentic Media
9 Holdom Avenue, Bletchley, Milton Keynes, Bucks, MK1 1QR, UK
and PO Box 1047 Waynesboro, GA 30830-2047, USA
www.authenticmedia.co.uk

British Library Cataloguing in Publication Data

A catalogue record for this book is available from the British Library

ISBN 1-85078-605-4

Cover design by 4-9-0 ltd
Photography © Adam Greene and Keswick Convention Council
Print Management by Adare Carwin
Printed and Bound in Denmark by Nørhaven Paperback

Contents

The Bible Readings

The Lectures

The Addresses

Introduction by the Chairman of the 2004 Convention

Many of you reading this book will have been in attendance at the Convention last year. I'm sure it will serve as a great reminder of a wonderful three weeks of ministry and maybe of some particular word from God to you through that ministry.

Some of you may never have visited the Convention. I trust this book of Bible teaching will prove to be a real encouragement to you and might motivate you to attend the Convention in the future.

The purpose of the Keswick Convention and the satellite Conventions around the country and around the world, is to preach Christ and his lordship over our lives through the exposition of the word of God. On behalf of the Council of the Convention, I want to express my gratitude to all the preachers who did that so faithfully last summer and the great army of workers who made that preaching possible.

So we look forward to Keswick 2005 and our theme of 'The Glory of the Gospel.' Our prayer is that God himself will be glorified as we consider the great grace and mercy of the gospel and as we determine to live our lives in the power of that gospel. I look forward to meeting you there.

Sincerely in Christ,
Peter Maiden

Editor's Introduction

Another summer, another feast of Bible teaching, another series of difficult decisions to make! This volume contains not only many of the evening addresses, but the powerful series of Habakkuk, given in week 2 by Jonathan Lamb. We have also included, for the first time, all three of the Keswick lectures, all of which were superb.

Alistair Begg's Bible readings on Ruth will be published separately, as will the evening addresses given on Daniel in week 3 – both will be part of the Keswick Bible study guide series, together with Michael Baughen's Bible readings from the September Bible week, on Covenant.

Those of you who attended this year's Convention will know that Derek Tidball, the Principal of the London School of Theology, stepped in at almost the last minute to give the week 3 Bible readings, in place of Nigel Lee, who was taken ill. These Bible readings were based on a book Derek Tidball wrote recently for Christian Focus, *Wisdom from Heaven*.

I hope you all enjoy reading this book as much as I have enjoyed working on it!

Ali Hull

The Bible Readings

Why?

by Jonathan Lamb

JONATHAN LAMB

Jonathan is presently Director of Langham Preaching for Langham Partnership International, which is a global programme seeking to encourage a new generation of preachers and teachers. This is a ministry which networks with national leaders in many parts of the world, including Africa, Asia, Latin America as well as Central Europe and Eurasia. Formerly a chairman of both the Keswick Convention and Word Alive, Jonathan still serves as a Trustee of Keswick. He has written several books, including the recently published title for Keswick entitled *'Faith in the Face of Danger'*, based on his Bible readings from Nehemiah given in 2000. He is married to Margaret and they have three daughters.

Why?

Habakkuk 1:1–2:1

'Out of Control?' There is no doubt at all that the theme of the Convention this year resonates not only with Christians but taps into the mood of our culture. There is hardly a country around the world where this question is not surfacing. Who is in control? Who can you trust? There is a frightening array of uncertainties. *The Economist* publication, *The World in 2004*, summarises some of the possibilities and gives a handy checklist of potential disasters to look out for. SARS, for example, may reappear with a vengeance, so that the seven hundred or so deaths of last year will be insignificant, particularly if it takes hold in places like sub-Saharan Africa. Or if world recovery fails to take a hold, there is a prediction of worldwide recession. Then there is the sustained threat of from rogue states: if there is military engagement in North Korea or Iran, then the ripple effects will be global. And, most obviously, the threat of international terror: never mind the billions which people spend on defence and security systems, nothing can control this particular threat.

We sense that we have entered an era of bewildering uncertainty where no one is in control. It is a faultline in our culture, a deep vulnerability that many people express. It is not simply to do with global events. It is also as a concern that their own personal world seems out of control. I remember speaking to a pastor of a London church. He was seventy years old, fifty years a Christian, and had had a demanding pastoral responsibility in speaking to a young couple whose four-year-old daughter had died in tragic circumstances. It caused him to consider everything which he believed about suffering and the character of God. He was not bitter but he was deeply perplexed. Many of us confess to the same experience. We realise that there are many things in this world which appear to contradict a bland confidence in God.

We are going to see from the story of Habakkuk that authentic biblical spirituality looks at these hard realities in the face. Habakkuk insists that this is God's world and that he is actively involved in it. All of us, sooner or later, confront a point of tension between what we believe about God's goodness and character and what we observe in the real world around us. Often we discover that our experience does not match our belief. We can live shallow Christian lives by keeping those two worlds apart. We refuse to allow a two-way conversation between the difficult questions of our world and the certainties of our faith and we somehow imagine that faith is like that schoolboy definition, 'Faith is believing in things that ain't true.' What we believe and what goes on in the real world do not seem to match.

This point of tension is frequently presented to us in the Bible, whether in the wisdom literature, Job, Ecclesiastes, the Psalms, or the prophets. It's exactly the experience of Habakkuk. For like all prophets, Habakkuk brings the word of God to the people; but what is especially interesting is that he also speaks *our* words to God. He confronts God with his confusion and speaks for us. Is God really in control? As he looked at the bewildering circumstances in which he lived, how could Habakkuk be sure that this God was the God of the universe who was on the throne? As far as he was concerned, God had made so many promises to his people, that through them *'all the families of the earth would be blessed'*, and yet they did not seem to be coming true. Habakkuk's name could mean 'to embrace', which is expressive of the way he took the pains and sorrows of his people to heart. It might also hint at his own wrestling with God, as he struggled with perplexing questions of all kinds.

Yet Habakkuk is a book about God's purposes for his people and his world. In the course of three chapters we will see how God brings the prophet to understand that reality. But chapter 1 begins with a dialogue between Habakkuk and the Lord, dominated by the question: 'Why?' The dialogue has three main sections.

1. Habakkuk's problem (Hab. 1:1–4)

Carrying a burden (verse 1)

That's the literal translation of the opening word of the prophecy, 'The oracle that Habakkuk the prophet received' (verse 1). It is 'the burden' he received. Here was a man with a heavy load on his heart and mind. Like all of the prophets, he receives a word from the Lord, but the burden is also related to his burdened heart. It is very expressive of how he feels about what is happening in his own country, amongst his own people. It is there in the opening words (verses 3, 4). 'Why...?'

'Who is in control?' Habakkuk was overwhelmed by that question. He was living in Jerusalem, in the final days of the seventh century BC, after the reign of King Josiah. King Josiah was the great king, the one who had introduced all kinds of reforms. He had had a conversion experience as a young man, he had discovered the law, pulled down the pagan altars and restored the Temple. There was prosperity as God blessed the nation. But he was followed by King Jehoiakim who succeeded in reversing all of the good work. Under his reign the people ignored God's laws. They still expected God to bless them: after all, they were *his* people. But they ignored his law and gradually a terrible decline set in.

This is when Habakkuk was living. He was watching the slide away from God. So too was Jeremiah, who was prophesying at the same time. Notice the language of his cry in verses 3, 4. 'Violence' is a word repeated many times in these first two chapters. It was a completely lawless society, shaped by the determination of people to forget what God had said and to live life on their own terms. They disobeyed his law, and prophets and priests alike were hopelessly compromised. As verse 4 expresses it, 'Therefore the law is paralysed'. God's word was frozen out. There was no justice at all. King Jehoiakim built his wonderful palaces, exploited the people, and showed no repentance, no mercy. And so the priests, politicians and civil servants took their cue from the king, demonstrating the same injustice. No wonder that Habakkuk says, 'The wicked hem in the righteous' (verse 4). The few who did hang on to the word of the Lord, the righteous, were completely surrounded. Why was God allowing his people to act like this? Why was God making him look at it? It was a burden of disappointment, disillusionment, almost despair. Only God could help in this situation.

Calling for help (verses 2–4)

That is the second feature of these opening verses. He wrestles with the problem and with God. There is an intensity in the way in which these words are written. The words imply he shouts, screams, roars even, 'Help, Lord! Why is your law being trampled on? Why are you allowing people to drift away?' The real crisis for Habakkuk was that he cried again and again, but it seemed God was not listening (verse 2). 'How long?' 'Why?' Those two questions are often on our lips. After you have been calling for a long time, it is hard to avoid the conclusion that God can't be interested. Why is justice flouted? Why pray? Why have faith? Why is it all such a burden? As far as Habakkuk was concerned, everything seemed out of joint. It wasn't just the sinfulness of the people that was the problem – that was bad enough – but it was his suspicion that God's delay in disciplining his people was somehow a blot on God's righteous character.

It was not an intellectual problem so much as a deeply-felt pain for Habakkuk. These questions aren't academic questions. It was a painful burden for Habakkuk. For many people, any explanation is better than silence. At such times, it is very important to do what

Habakkuk does: to admit our bewilderment. Christians are allowed to do that. Evangelicals often have great difficulty in living with such bewildering questions, living with mystery. I wonder too if we have the same sense of burden as we look at our own Christian community? Or are we lulled into an easy-going acceptance of the status quo, a spiritual apathy which can so easily set in amongst God's people? I wonder if we have the same agony of spirit and honesty before God? It was Habakkuk's understanding of God that led him to shout out this complaint, 'If this is true about you God, then why aren't you acting, why the delay?'

2. God's purpose (verses 5–11)

Now God replies. This section begins with the word 'Look' (verse 5), which picks up Habakkuk's complaint in verse 3, 'Why do you make me look at injustice?' God says, 'Take a wider look. Look at the nations and watch – and be utterly amazed. For I am going to do something in your days that you would not believe, even if you were told'. That is exactly what Habakkuk needed to do, and often what we need to do: to gain God's wider perspective. Notice two important features of God's reply to the questions that Habakkuk has posed.

God is at work (verse 5)

First, God had heard Habakkuk's prayer. God was already at work. God was not standing by, indifferent to the concerns which Habakkuk was putting forward. No, he says 'I am already at work if only you had eyes to see it.' The Lord is behind a series of devastating events that would change the course of history in Habakkuk's day. He has not abandoned his plans. Judah and all of the nations are still under God's watchful eye and he is raising up a solution to the problem which so concerned Habakkuk. 'I am raising up the Babylonians, that ruthless and impetuous people, who sweep across the whole earth to seize dwelling-places not their own. They are a feared and dreaded people; they are a law to themselves and promote their own honour. ... They deride kings and scoff at rulers. They laugh at all fortified cities ... guilty men, whose own strength is their god' (verses 6,7,10,11). That description of the devastation which the Babylonians were about to bring on God's own people wouldn't be out of place in our world. The Babylonians were guilty of international terrorism, ethnic cleansing, ruthless power. This was 'a great military juggernaut' which crushed everything in its power.

The Lord's reply to Habakkuk's complaint that he was indifferent is: 'Let me show you that I am working in ways which you would hardly believe if it were told you' (verse 5). Sometimes we have particular expectations of how God ought to work in our lives, how he should answer our prayers. Do you remember Paul's testimony in Philippians 1? He was stuck in prison but he says 'I want you to know, brothers, that what has happened to me has really served to advance the gospel' (Phil. 1:12). The frontline of the gospel is being pushed forward. How was that possible? Paul says 'For one thing, every day one of Caesar's personal bodyguards is there chained to me. Four teams of four soldiers throughout the day – it's a captive audience.' Paul realised the gospel could reach social circles in Nero's time that it never would have reached had it not been for his imprisonment. He went on to say that other Christians were encouraged to preach the word of God more courageously because of his imprisonment. He had the eyes to see that there was another story: God was at work.

That is exactly the perspective that some of us need. Many of you come from very small churches in demanding situations. Some of you come from countries where the church is under enormous pressure. We should not lose sight of this first reality in God's reply: 'I am at work.'

God is in control (verse 6)

The second reality in God's reply is that he is in control. Verse 6, 'I am raising up the Babylonians'. God is not only at work but he will do so according to his own plans and purposes. Many years ago, Martyn Lloyd-Jones wrote a little commentary on Habakkuk, called *From fear to faith*. Lloyd-Jones says this about the Babylonians: 'God had unexpected providences and unusual instruments.' You are not kidding, Habakkuk would have said! This would be part of his perplexity. God was implying that it was going to get a lot worse before it would get better. What was troubling for Habakkuk was that although the Babylonians were in the driving seat of this great war machine, God was the commander. Why was God doing this? God's people had ignored his justice so Babylonian justice would be what they would receive. God's people were characterised by destruction and violence and so God says, 'Violence is what you will have.'

The Babylonians were not just under God's sovereign authority, they were an instrument for God's purpose. These verses underline a very profound truth: God is the God of history. God is even the God of such ruthless powers in our world. He is in control of the movements even of pagan nations. Calvin commented on these verses, 'It isn't by their own instinct but by the hidden impulse of God … God can employ the vices of men in executing his judgements. The wicked are led here and there by the hidden power of God.' It might have seemed that it was the military prowess of the Babylonians which would eventually result in their success. But it was God who had raised them up. God is in control.

It is vital that this truth settles in our heads and hearts. Exactly the same principle appears in the New Testament. The early Christians were bewildered at what had happened with Jesus' death. In their prayer meeting in Acts 4, they state that Herod, Pontius Pilate, the Gentiles and the people of Israel had conspired against Jesus. But then they add (Acts 4:28), [But] They did what your power and will decided beforehand should happen.' The early Christians realised that the events in Jerusalem when Jesus was crucified weren't events that were completely out of control. There was another story. It was God's power, God's will, God's decision.

The book of Job underlines exactly the same point. God granted permission to Satan to test Job and God set the boundaries. As David Atkinson has pointed out, although there is evil in the story of Job, there is not dualism. Some Christians appear to live their lives as if they were in a *Star Wars* adventure, surrounded by equal and opposite forces of good and evil. Neither good nor evil is quite strong enough and so that event must be God's and this event must be the devil. It is almost as if there are two worlds of good and evil, with our lives swinging between the two. That is not the picture that the Bible gives us. God is always in control, always sovereign. Satan himself is under God's control, as the book of Job tells us. Habakkuk 1 underlines that reality. God is saying 'I am the one behind human history.' The Babylonians might think they are in control. The Brits, the Americans might think they are in control. Al Quaeda might think they are in control. But the rise and the fall of nations, empires, dictators and terrorists is in God's hands.

We often comment on the way in which this is seen in global events such as the Communist takeover of China in the 1950s, when thousands of missionaries were evacuated but which, in God's good purposes, resulted in extraordinary growth of the church, in ways that never would have been predicted.

It is also true in the midst of personal tragedy. Just a few weeks ago, I was with a friend of mine, Ivan, in India. He was speaking about the way in which the church in India has been growing remarkably over the past few years. There were a number of reasons for the growth but significantly, he said, two woman ought to be mentioned. One was Mother Teresa and the other was Gladys Staines. Mrs Staines was until recently still serving the Lord in India. Her husband Graham was an Australian missionary, working amongst lepers and tribal peoples in Orissa in North India. In January 1999 he and his two sons were killed whilst in a vehicle that was set on fire by a mob. His grieving widow, Gladys, told the newspaper reporter the following morning: 'I am deeply upset but I am not angry for Jesus has taught us how to love our enemies.' Her words were carried in all of the Indian dailies, across the country and outside of India as well, and hundreds of people asked the question 'Why are you Christians different?' Ivan charts the remarkable growth of the church back to that witness, that tragedy.

Vinoth Ramachandra has said this: 'I cannot help feeling that a middle-aged Australian widow has done more for the cause of the gospel in India than all of the slick evangelists on the 24-hour channel networks now beaming into that country.' There was no question at all that the family, or the church, were overwhelmed with the grief of that appalling tragedy. Many people have thought long and hard about how God's purposes could possibly be fulfilled through it. Some of us may be walking along a similar path. Events occur and we cannot make sense of them. How on earth can God be working and in control? Yet that's what Habakkuk chapter 1 says, that's what Acts 4 says, that's what Job says, that's what Gladys Staines is saying. God is at work, God is in control.

3. Habakkuk's perplexity (verses 12–17)

Habakkuk could hardly believe his ears. And neither could the people in Jerusalem. One of the worst aspects of their treachery was they had lulled themselves into a false sense of security. 'We are God's people.' They could not believe that God would judge them through the Babylonians. It's very easy for religious people, like us, to become careless, even to mock the idea that God could judge them. Evangelicals may sometimes be in danger of that kind of flippancy.

But God was going to fulfil his word. That's the issue throughout the book of Habakkuk. If he promises blessings to those who obey, that's what he will do. If he promises judgement to those who disobey, that will happen as well. But that wasn't Habakkuk's problem. He had been asking for judgement. He had another problem – instead of God's purposes being achieved or advanced, it seems to Habakkuk to be going in exactly the opposite direction. The cure seemed worse than the illness. It's the point of tension which I mentioned at the very beginning. You see the apparent conflict in verses 12 and 13. Verse 12 is what he believes; by contrast, verse 13 is what he observes.

a) Confidence (verses 12,13)

Many of the psalmists and prophets set their hard questions in the context of their certainties. That's very important for our Christian lives. You have all kinds of questions but ask those questions in the midst of your certainties. That's exactly what Habakkuk does. He expresses his confidence in three ways.

God's commitment First, Habakkuk underlines God's commitment. He says, 'My God, my Holy One' (verse 12). 'You are the faithful, covenant-keeping God, I belong to you.' Habakkuk affirms that fundamental certainty. 'We will not die', he says. That's exactly our confidence too. God will not let go of us. We belong to him, whatever happens. God is not going to give up on his faithful people.

God's eternity In this turbulent world which Habakkuk lived in, he was certain of another reality. God is eternal (verse 12). 'O LORD, are you not from everlasting?' He is the God who is engaged in history but he is above all of the turbulent ebb and flow. Whatever the fears and uncertainties of our lives, God is the Eternal, the Everlasting. He is the Rock (verse 12), the one stable element in this uncertain world. If things are shaking in our lives, we need to hold onto God's changelessness.

God's purpose Verse 12, 'O LORD, you have appointed them to execute judgement; O Rock, you have ordained them to punish.' Habakkuk realises that the coming Babylonian invasion is something which God has ordained. Other prophets, like Ezekiel, Jeremiah and Isaiah, also realised that international events are not random. They are all part of God's sovereign purpose. That's his third expression of confidence.

I think that is enormously important in our own lives. I give one illustration, which for me is descriptive of the Christian life. It comes from my first experience of sailing, off the Sound of Mull in Scotland, one summer some years back. It was an incredible summer until we arrived in Scotland. The winds rose to almost storm-force, but the skipper was determined that we would make the journey, and we learned how to beat against the wind. You go in one direction, and then tack, and then back in a sustained zig-zag movement. You make very slow progress but the remarkable thing is this: you are using the winds which are against you to make progress.

That is the most realistic model of the Christian life that I can think of. Sometimes Christians think we must always be riding high on some success-orientated spirituality. Jesus never promised us that. He did promise that whatever winds and waves are thrown at us, we will still make progress to our destination. That is God's purpose for our lives. We belong to him. He is the everlasting Lord. He is at work. He is in control. It's true at the international level. It's true at the personal level.

b) Contradiction (verses 13b–17)

But there is a point of tension and that is expressed in Habakkuk's perplexity from verse 13 onwards. He is bewildered by God's reply and I use the word contradiction to describe this. If his earlier complaint, in the early part of chapter 1, is that God is indifferent or inactive, then now his complaint is that God is inconsistent. Look at verse 13, 'Your eyes are too pure to look upon evil; you cannot tolerate wrong. Why then do you tolerate the treacherous? Why are you silent while the wicked swallow up those more righteous than themselves?' Look at the instrument that God has chosen! If God is meant to be the God of awesome purity, why does he allow the ruthless Babylonians to do their worst? If he uses them, he must be like them, as someone might put it. The imagery of verses 14 to 17 underlines their ruthless behaviour.

Sometimes it seems like that to us, too, in the perplexity of personal tragedies. It seems to contradict our understanding of God's character. Habakkuk's perpexity is not that he thinks judgement is unnecessary; he knows that judgement must come. His concern is: how can all of this possibly fulfil God's purposes of righteousness? How is God going to make it work out in terms of his promises of blessing? How long is all of this going to last? 'Is he to keep on emptying his net, destroying nations without mercy?' (verse 17). Is God going to allow this to go on for ever? When will his order finally be established?

This leads him to wait for God's answer, to which we will turn in chapter 2. But we close with three simple conclusions arising from chapter 1.

Christian spirituality

The demanding chapter we have looked at highlights three features of true spirituality.

Confronting reality

I realise that the issues of this book and chapter aren't always easy for us to face up to. We can resolve the tension that we have been speaking about by dividing our life into little boxes, with our Christian life over here, our faith over here and the rest of the world over here. We allow no two-way conversation. We keep our faith well away from the troubling questions of our world. Our faith is carefully protected. But without confronting those questions, the big issues and troubling doubts, faith very quickly degenerates into a kind of flabby, sentimental gullibility. There is no need to protect Christian faith in this way. Facing up to the tension enables us to find solid rock underneath, and adult godliness is characterised by such realism. Jim Packer, in his book *Knowing God*, says, 'Unreality towards God is the wasting disease of much modern Christianity. We need God to make us realists both about ourselves and about God.'

Praying honestly

Habakkuk 1 shows us that we should be willing for an honest dialogue with God. I like the way John Goldingay expresses it in one of his books. He says, 'We need not attempt to bottle it up because God invites us to pour it out.' That is what Habakkuk is about. That is what Jeremiah is about. That's what so many of the psalmists say to us. God invites us to pour it out, not to bottle it up. It is false spirituality to imagine that we must not ask these questions. If we try and exhibit a brave and cheerful face before other Christians or even before God, when inwardly we feel torn apart, it's almost certain to accentuate the condition. It's a mark of mature spirituality to confess these things to God. 'This is not merely an emotional catharsis', Goldingay says, 'like crying one's heart out in an empty room or losing one's temper and taking it out on the cushions. It is more adult to say what one feels to the person one regards as responsible.'

Habakkuk is not afraid to do that. He does not seem to hesitate to be quite straight with God.

Affirming certainty

Verse 12, 'My God, my Holy One, … [my] Rock'. Habakkuk is doing just what the psalmist does in Psalm 42. He raises the same kinds of questions, 'I will say to God, "My rock, why have you forgotten me for you are the God of my strength?"' And Martyn Lloyd-Jones' book on *Spiritual Depression* says this 'The essence of wisdom is to talk to yourself, not to listen to yourself.' That is, to repeat the certainties of God's word, the rock-solid affirmations of faith. When you are in this situation, it's very easy for questions and doubts to be overwhelming. So we remind ourselves of the certainties of God's word. We repeat to ourselves those confident realities that we have looked at. Habakkuk was a man of solid faith, honest faith. If we do the same, even in the blackest of moments, we will discover, as he did, that God is our refuge and strength. God is the everlasting Lord.

Wait!

Habakkuk 2:1–5

Some while ago, I spoke with a colleague of mine who said, 'The only thing holding me together is perpetual motion.' She meant that life had become so pressurised that if she were to stop, she would collapse. It's part of what is called 'modernity stress' – being obliged to squeeze more and more into less and less time. The idea of 'waiting' these days is completely counter-cultural. We are addicted to speed; we demand the instant. We are never 'out' any more; we are always in, always accessible, always available. Finding the opportunity to step aside from the distracted restlessness of our world or of our hearts is extremely difficult, but it is absolutely essential for the life of faith.

I work with Langham Partnership, with Chris Wright and John Stott, and there is a cottage in Pembrokeshire where we sometimes retreat, miles from anywhere, perched on a cliff that overlooks the sea. I was there, just myself, Habakkuk and about thirty sheep the other day, trying to retreat and reflect, pray and study. Then a couple of men arrived, doing some work on the buildings. One said to me 'This is a fantastic place. Not a soul around, absolutely peaceful ... very quiet ... But there's one thing you need, mate ... Sky television.'

That's our world. It's easy to be consumed by the day to day, to be swamped by the detail, so that your life is bounded by the horizons of your own activities. We need moments when we refresh our vision, gain that wider perspective. That's important in any form of Christian service but especially important when we are confronting some of the challenges to faith that we introduced yesterday from Habakkuk chapter 1.

From the human perspective, so much of what we do, even as believers, seems to be completely futile. When we compare our work as Christians to the scale of international turmoil or the opposition to the Christian faith which is raging in many parts of the world, or to the fragility of the Christian community – the whole things looks so futile. This is where Habakkuk restores our perspective. From chapter 2 verse 1 Habakkuk begins to gain a vision of God and his purposes in the world.

We will look just at these first five verses of chapter 2, and I would like to suggest three basic disciplines which Habakkuk learned, which will enable us to live lives of quiet trust in the middle of this crazy world.

1. Careful listening

After all of the turbulent questions and perplexed doubts of chapter 1, we begin with Habakkuk's determined resolve in verse 1: 'I will stand at my watch ... I will look to see what he will say to me'. Like other prophets, Habakkuk uses the idea of the watchman standing on the ramparts above the city of Jerusalem. He leaves the city behind, climbs the walls and longs for a renewed vision, a restored perspective. There he waits. Many of us find that the challenges of our world can sometimes obliterate our view of God. In fact, it wasn't just a change of view that Habakkuk was after. He was desperate to hear God's word. He longed to know what was happening in his world. As a man of faith, he believed in God's purposes, in God's control, but he was living in between the time when the promises were made and the time when the promises would be fulfilled. He was in the waiting room. That's exactly where we are. God has made so many promises. What will be the outcome?

Before we comment on the specific features of careful listening that are clear from verse 1, maybe you are thinking that this particular feature of Habakkuk's spiritual life seems incompatible with what we saw in chapter 1. Here he is quietly, patiently, listening. It seems a million miles away from all of the turbulent questions in chapter 1. In fact, these two things belong together. On the one hand, he pours out his heart to God. On the other, he waits on God. These are the two poles of prayer, and it's very helpful to see that they both co-exist in the same man. Habakkuk, after pouring it out, turns away from all of the distractions and waits on God. It must have been enormously difficult for him to have done that. Remember what was going on in Jerusalem: the violence and injustice. But it was vital that he stepped away and now heard God's voice.

A psalm that parallels this story is Psalm 73, where the psalmist is saying exactly the same as Habakkuk did in chapter 1. Why is it that the wicked always seem to succeed and the righteous suffer? Why, God, do you allow this to continue? Then the psalmist says in verses 16 and 17, 'When I tried to understand all this, it was oppressive to me till I entered the sanctuary of God; then I understood their final destiny.' Like Habakkuk, he took time to come into God's presence, and it was then that his perspective changed.

To what extent is this a feature of our own lives? I wonder if you identify with some of the questions that we looked at in chapter 1 and what your response is to those challenges? Sometimes we live more by the maxim, 'Why pray, when you can worry?' Committing these perplexities to God is one of the most important disciplines in our lives.

So what does careful listening really mean? There are three features worth noting.

a) An expectant faith (verse 1)

This verse implies an active, earnest waiting for God's word. But it also implies a measure of perseverance. He is standing, waiting for that word. These are very important qualities in our spiritual lives, whether we are reading God's word or praying. There is very little to be gained from reading the Bible without that kind of expectancy. Jesus' own ministry was frustrated when there was no expectancy on the part of his hearers. He began to teach in the synagogue and he was met by cynicism and incredulity. Expectant faith is the soil in which God's word will bear fruit, and we need to persevere in this discipline.

Remember what we saw in chapter 1. Although he felt the weariness of it all (verse 2), he kept on persevering with expectant faith, believing that God would finally speak his word. Don Carson says 'Pray until you pray … Christians should pray long enough and honestly enough at a single session to get past the feeling of formalism and unreality that attends a little praying. Many of us in our praying are like nasty little boys who ring the front door bells and run away before anyone answers.' Pray until you finally believe you are praying.

b) A submissive spirit (verse 1)

Note the end of verse 1. 'I will look to see what he will say to me, and what answer I am to give to this complaint.' In the NIV there is an alternative reading which says, 'what to answer when I am rebuked.' It could read, 'I will look to see what he will say to me, and the correction that I am going to receive.' He was aware of how bold he had been in God's presence in chapter 1. It is almost shocking to see the way in which he addressed God with his complaints, his anxious questions, and so now, as he comes up on the city ramparts, he realises he must be ready for the Lord's rebuke, the Lord's discipline, 'the correction that I receive.' He had presented all of the arguments, so now he is submissive enough to wait for reproof.

I like David Prior's observation in the *Bible Speaks Today*: 'God looks not just for honesty but he also looks for humility.' Coming into God's presence with patient listening requires that we adopt the same stance. In all prayer, we must be submissive as well as honest, ready for what God is going to say to us, open to any reproof or discipline that may be necessary. Maybe you have heard the story of an announcement that was made in a missionary magazine concerning the former General Director of a particular mission who was retiring, but was going to continue to serve the Lord 'in an advisory capacity.' We are not the ones with the answers when it comes to praying. We are not in control. Coming into God's presence in the way in which Habakkuk did requires that we are 'teachable as well as frank', as David Prior puts it; submissive as well as honest, open to listen. The Lord will change our lives if we come into his presence with this kind of patient listening. That was certainly the case for Habakkuk.

c) A responsive heart

'Then the LORD replied: "Write down the revelation:…"' (verse 2). The key thing in these verses is that word 'revelation' – that's where the emphasis is resting. It is God's revealed word that Habakkuk receives, and which he is told to write down so that the herald may run with it. The word of revelation, of course, is the vital turning point for Habakkuk. If we are perplexed about what is happening in the church, or the uncertainties of the world, or the dilemmas in our own lives, then the starting point is to strengthen our confidence in God's revelation, his authoritative word to us. And not just the prophecy of Habakkuk but the entire revelation that God has given us in Scripture. We are here in Keswick because we believe God's word matters. God's word is authoritative, powerful, dynamic and life-giving. We are here to look at that word, 'to see what he will say to me' (verse 1). Throughout its pages Scripture urges us to have responsive hearts.

What is your hearing like? I don't mean the state of your inner ear or your auditory nerve. What about your spiritual sensitivity, your ability to hear God's voice? God is a speaking God, and a speaking God calls for a listening people. Throughout the Bible, hearing God's voice is a very urgent matter. There is a very insistent piece of writing in Hebrews, chapter 3, where the writer quotes from Psalm 95 several times: 'So, as the Holy Spirit says: "Today, if you hear his voice, do not harden your hearts ..."' (Heb. 3:7,8).

Calvin's commentary on this section of Habakkuk reads like this: 'As long as we judge according to our own perceptions, we walk on the earth, and while we do so, many clouds arise and Satan scatters ashes in our eyes and wholly darkens our judgement, and thus is happens that we lie down altogether confounded. It is hence wholly necessary that we should tread our reason underfoot, and come nigh to God himself. Let the word of God become our ladder'. It is a very beautiful expression and it expresses exactly what Habakkuk did. That is our task as well: to let the word of God become the ladder into God's presence, above the turmoil of this world, so that we hear his word, listen to his will and purpose in Scripture, and determine to obey it.

Many of us find this a real challenge. In line with the values of our culture, we prefer instant results instead of the challenge of reading and understanding and applying the word of God. But if we are to find stability in this uncertain world, this is precisely what we must do. If we are going to live by faith, we must have responsive hearts to his word.

Let me quote something with which I strongly identify. John White writes in one of his books —

> Bible study has torn apart my life and remade it. That is to say that God, through his word, has done so. In the darkest periods of my life, when everything seemed hopeless, I would struggle in the grey dawns of many faraway countries to grasp the basic truths of Scripture passages. I looked for no immediate answer to my problems. Only did I sense intuitively that I was drinking draughts from a fountain that gave life to my soul. Slowly as I grappled with the theological problems, a strength grew deep within me, foundations cemented themselves to an other-worldly rock, beyond the reach of time and space, and I became strong and more alive. If I could write poetry about it I would. If I could sing through paper, I would flood your soul with the glorious melodies that express what I have found. I cannot exaggerate, for there are no expressions majestic enough to tell

of the glory I have seen, or of the wonder of finding that I, a neurotic, unstable, middle-aged man, have my feet firmly planted in eternity and breathe the air of heaven. And all this has come to me through a careful study of Scripture.

Note the seriousness of what God says to Habakkuk about this revelation. 'Write down the revelation and make it plain on tablets so that the herald may run with it' (verse 2). Writing on tablets is expressive of the seriousness of this word of revelation. This is the message that needs to be preserved; it's of lasting importance. It may also have been necessary to record it on stone tablets because it would be some while before the revelation would ultimately be fulfilled. So write it down, Habakkuk is told; make sure it's recorded. This is a serious message. Maybe the recording on tablets also brought to mind the tablets of the Ten Commandments. This is the vital word from God. Perhaps the phrase also emphasises urgency, as if the Lord were saying, 'Mark my words, Habakkuk. This word will come to pass.'

He has to make it plain, verse 2 says, so that everyone can understand the significance of this revelation. It should be passed on to others. This message is for all; take this word seriously. This is where our hearts and minds are going to be shaped according to God's perspective.

Eugene Peterson, writing about the book of Jeremiah, says

If we forget that the newspapers are footnotes to Scripture and not the other way round, we will finally be afraid to get out of bed in the morning. The meaning of the world is most accurately given to us by God's Word.

2. Patient waiting (verse 3)

Waiting is not something we are particularly good at in our culture, is it? How are you waiting at the checkout in Tescos? Or in a traffic jam? Waiting is not at all easy.

As we saw in chapter 1, waiting for God's actions, as far as Habakkuk was concerned, was excruciatingly painful. That's why he was asking: 'How long?' He was longing for God's purposes to be fulfilled. Like us, he was in the waiting room. When will God's promises finally be delivered? When will God's word be fulfilled? For many people the pain of waiting is one of the most severe tests in their Christian discipleship. Let's notice three things from the Lord's word in verse 3.

a) An appointed time (verse 3)

Habakkuk was tempted to ask if God was true to his promises, if God had forgotten his covenant people. In chapter 1 he is reminded that God was at work, and here in verse 3 the Lord repeats the message. There is 'an appointed time' when God's word will be fulfilled.

We should not imagine that this world is out of control. God's word and God's promise will be fulfilled. There is an appointed time. He is in control of the course of history. The appointed time in verse 3 is actually a specific moment. It is the alarm bell ringing. The ESV says: 'It hastens to the end'; the word used there is the word from breathing. It's as if this word is panting, yearning for the end, gasping like a runner heading for the finishing line.

Habakkuk can be absolutely sure that what God now declares about the coming judgement of his people will take place. That's the first circle of application, the immediate context. And, sure enough, it happened. They were carted off into exile just as Jeremiah predicted. But the word of judgement was also fulfilled in the Babylonians, who were the tool in God's hand to bring about that initial judgement. The ruthless Babylonians would also be judged. God's word had an appointed time for them as well. And we can go out in further concentric circles to the ultimate end, when God will finally act in judgement. Habakkuk is looking outwards even to what the Old Testament calls the Day of the Lord, to what the New Testament refers to as the Day of Christ.

If you are tempted, like Habakkuk, to think that God must have abandoned his people or given up on his promises, then we too must remember to wait patiently, because 'the revelation awaits an appointed time'. I realise that this is often rather cold comfort for people who are going through difficulties. It doesn't always help for heart-broken people to be told: 'Hang on. It's going to get better.' But from a pastoral perspective it is very important to try and retain the longer term perspective. There is an appointed time. God is not mocking us with his word.

In his book *The Christian Mind*, Harry Blamires said, 'A prime mark of the Christian mind is that it cultivates the eternal perspective. It looks beyond this life to another one. It is supernaturally orientated and brings to bear upon earthly considerations the fact of heaven and the fact of hell.' In other words, it sees things as they really are.

Hebrews 11 reminds us that Moses was exactly the same. He was 'looking ahead to his reward' (verse 26). The verb that is used means 'to fix your eyes on something', like an artist intently gazing at the portrait he is painting. Faith that makes a difference is faith that fixes its eyes on the ultimate, not just the immediate. Take the long view. God has today and tomorrow under his control.

b) A reliable message (verse 3)

'[It] will not prove false' (verse 3). This follows from the fact that it is God who is speaking. God cannot lie so neither does the revelation. There is an absolute certainty about that word. From where he stood above Jerusalem on that day, appearances certainly seemed to contradict that message of God's ultimate control. But the Lord affirms, 'it will not lie.'

Peter was going to say exactly the same to the cynical people of his day. People doubted that the Lord would ever come back, that God would ever deliver on the promises that he made. And so Peter stresses that what God had said was absolutely reliable. When God spoke in creation it produced results; when God spoke in judgement there was the flood; and by that same word he will judge in the future (2 Pet. 3:2-7). He does not lie. It is a reliable message. Isaiah uses a simple picture in Isaiah 55 of the water cycle – the rain falls, achieves its purpose and then returns. As in the natural world, so in the spiritual world. When God sends his word, it achieves its purpose. 'It … will accomplish what I desire and achieve the purpose for which I sent it' (Is. 55:11). Little by little, then, Habakkuk is learning that God is in control. It is a reliable message.

c) It will not delay (verse 3)

Thirdly, the Lord reinforces the certainty of the outcome by declaring, 'Though it linger, wait for it; it will certainly come and will not delay' (verse 3). In the context of patient waiting, this speaks to one of our challenges: our timescale and God's timescale. Do you remember how Peter expressed it to those who were asking 'why isn't God acting'? Peter quotes from Psalm 90, 'With the Lord a day is like a thousand years, and a thousand years are like a day' (2 Pet. 3:8). The delay in God's actions might seem long, but God sees time with a perspective that we lack. A long time for us isn't necessarily a long time for God.

We forget the great stories of Moses and his 40 years in the wilderness, or the delay of 20 years before Joseph was vindicated. But as we walk with the Lord, we begin to learn this lesson – looking back with a longer perspective we learn to appreciate that God's time is best. Peter is referring to God's ultimate timescale which will end with a new heaven and a new earth. The vantage point from the end radically affects our perspective on the present. That's the nature of Christian hope. The reality of that ultimate future radically transforms the way we live here and now.

Christians can formally subscribe to the doctrine of heaven but live practically as though this world were all there is. We can live as though there were no tomorrow. Let me quote John Stott in a comment on Psalm 73, 'If the men and women of this world live in the cramped quarters of time, we Christians should learn to inhabit the wide open spaces of eternity'.

3. Steadfast believing (verses 4 and 5)

The third main theme to which we turn is a profound turning point in Habakkuk's prophecy. The issue for Habakkuk, and for all believers, is this: how do we live in the meantime, in the waiting room? We are going to look at the key verse of the whole book. It is a verse which acts as the watershed in relation not just to the story here but in relation to all men and women. Indeed, it is the watershed for all of the nations because it gives us the two alternatives: faith or unbelief. 'See, he is puffed up; his desires are not upright – but the righteous will live by his faith' (verse 4). It sets the context for the whole book. It marks the contrast between the righteous who trust God and who are faithful and, on the other hand, the proud, bloodthirsty Babylonians. It speaks of the contrasted motives of true and false living, of the godly and the ungodly, the Christian perspective and the pagan perspective.

The reply that Habakkuk receives in these verses, through his careful listening and his patient waiting, is the ultimate solution to all of the problems he has expressed. God's purposes will be worked out in history. The ultimate fate of the righteous and of the wicked may be slow in appearing, but the outcome is absolutely certain. Evil will be overthrown. God's enemies will be punished. In the meantime, the righteous have to keep on trusting God. Let's look at the two possible attitudes.

Unbelief (verses 4,5)

Habakkuk's description of the ungoldly is in verse 4. 'See, he is puffed up; his desires are not upright.' Such people are inflated with pride. They are completely self-reliant and that, of course, is why they are unable to find a righteousness outside of themselves. They live their lives in a completely self-contained way. They think they need nothing. It's quite the opposite of Jesus' opening Beatitude: 'Blessed are those who know their need of God.' They certainly don't, so by definition, they can't be upright.

Look at verse 5, 'indeed, wine betrays him; he is arrogant and never at rest. Because he is as greedy as the grave and like death is never satisfied, he gathers to himself all the nations and takes captive all the peoples.' Such people have deluded themselves. Proud and arrogant, they are never at rest. One translation says, 'he is never at home.' He is restless with his consuming ambition to get more. Nothing will satisfy him. Verse 5 explains that, like death itself, he just can't get enough. There is an echo of the description of the Babylonians in chapter 1, swallowing up nations to satisfy their greedy appetite (verses 15–17).

So we are given a sketch in verses 4 and 5 of what we'll see in the rest of chapter 2. It's a picture of the self-contained, self-obsessed person who shakes his little fist at God and says, 'I have no need of you.' Such a person is living a lie.

Faith (verse 4)

'But the righteous will live by his faith' (verse 4). The righteous are those who steadily look to God, who are committed to him. Their life is characterised by steady perseverance, trusting in God and his purposes. They live by faith, not by sight.

Habakkuk's phrase is used in several New Testament passages to express the heart of the gospel. In Romans 1 Paul describes how all have sinned, all deserve God's judgement, and all have the opportunity to respond to the gospel. Justification is based not on what we do, but it is by faith in Jesus Christ alone, for Jew and Gentile alike. 'For in the gospel a righteousness from God is revealed, a righteousness that is by faith from first to last, just as it is written, ' "The righteous will live by faith." ' (Rom. 1:17). The way of the gospel is the exact opposite to the attitude represented by the self-sufficient unbeliever that is expressed in Habakkuk 2. When we come to God, we must come knowing that we have nothing whatsoever to contribute to our salvation. Emil Brunner once said, 'All other religions but the gospel save us the ultimate humiliation of being stripped naked before God.'

Habakkuk came to see that the attitude of steadfast faith was the only way to live. The righteous, by his faith, shall live. It is to recognise that the whole of your life is in the hands of God. The writer to the Hebrews also quotes from Habakkuk 2:4, demonstrating that such faith is a matter of perseverance, waiting for what God has promised (Heb. 10:35–39). 'He who is coming will come and will not delay', says the writer, changing Habakkuk 2:3 from 'it' to 'him' – 'he who is coming will not delay'! Faith is a matter of holding on to the Lord Jesus, looking for his return.

Faith not only involves the initial act of believing when we receive the gospel of God's grace. It is also the steady perseverance of faithfulness. We depend entirely on him. We are to live day by day under this controlling principle, that God is absolutely true to what he has said. That is the issue. What is the controlling principle in your life and mine? What is my fundamental motivation? The word of the Lord to Habakkuk is that the only way to live is by wholehearted trust in the God who rules this entire universe.

I finish with the words of William McConnell, Deputy Governor of the Maze, in Northern Ireland, spoken shortly before he was assassinated. 'I have committed my life, talents, work and action to Almighty God, in the sure and certain knowledge that, however slight my hold of him may have been, his promises are sure and his hold on me complete.' The righteous will live by his faith.

Woe!

Habakkuk 2:6–20

There is an old Chinese proverb which goes like this: 'To prophesy is extremely difficult especially with regard to the future.' But actually there is no shortage of people trying to predict what our future holds. Some of them are surprisingly optimistic, but the vast majority of people who attempt to predict the future line up with the remark made by Arthur C. Clarke, well known for the movie *2001: A Space Odyssey*. He wrote: 'No age has shown more interest in the future than ours; which is ironic, since it may not have one.' Many people share his pessimism. There is now a deep-set uncertainty about what our future holds. We are no longer optimistic about the future of our planet, about international stability, about our own nation or even our own lives.

Perhaps this issue is one of the most significant in relation to our theme, 'Out of Control?'. How do we cope with the uncertainties and the pessimism which so easily eats away at the morale of people in our society, even in active Christian communities?

The issue at the heart of the book of Habakkuk, as we have seen, is the purpose of God. Will God fulfil all of the promises he has made? The rest of the prophecy from chapter 2 onwards is an assertion that all of history is being directed by God himself. So where is this world heading? What is going to happen to those people who shake their fists at God, who prefer to run life on their own terms? The next section of Habakkuk demonstrates that the Lord God, the Alpha and the Omega, sees the end from the beginning.

The first level of application in this section relates to Judah in Habakkuk's day. God's own people they may have been, but they carried no diplomatic immunity. Then the words of judgement are especially graphic in relation to the Babylonians. But we will also see something of 'the wheels of providence' as the judgement goes out beyond Judah, beyond the Babylonians, out ultimately to a judgement of all of those who refuse to live by faith in the Sovereign Lord.

The certainty of God's judgement

We will choose as our key word for this section, 'Woe', which appears five times in these verses, and is probably a multi-layered expression. It includes the idea of derision, almost as though the Lord is saying 'Ha! You think you are in charge, you are safe, you will win the glory. You've got another thing coming.' There are echoes of mocking laughter. Some think the word 'woe' also includes a sense of mourning, as in a funeral chant, whilst others suggest it implies the anger of a curse, as in Isaiah's phrase, 'Shame on you.'

This particular section is called a taunt song. One or two preachers rightly suggest that in our culture we are familiar with the idea of a taunt song. On a Saturday afternoon you can hear the taunt songs on the football terraces, as the supporters of one side jeer at the opposition. The focus of the song is the Babylonians, but we should hold in our minds the key verse in Habakkuk 2:4. If this verse sets out the two alternatives of faith and unbelief, it also hints at the two outcomes or destinies. The taunt song has something to say to all those who take their stand against God.

The 'woes of judgement' are not a particularly common theme in evangelical preaching, and as we turn to this chapter it is worth reflecting on our own reaction to the idea of judgement. Jim Packer wrote in his book *Knowing God*

> Do you believe in divine judgement? By which I mean, do you believe in a God who acts as our Judge? Many, it seems, do not. Speak to them of God as a Father, a friend, a helper, one who loves us despite all our weakness and folly and sin, and their faces light up; you are on their wavelength at once. But speak to them of God as Judge and they frown and shake their heads. Their minds recoil from such an idea. They find it repellent and unworthy. But there are few things stressed more strongly in the Bible than the reality of God's work as Judge.

Habakkuk didn't have that problem. That was part of the perplexity we saw in chapter 1. He wanted to see justice but he feared that people were going to be let off the hook, that God's justice was unreliable. Think about it for a moment. Most people, Christian and non-Christian, are looking for justice. You hear non-Christians say in the media, 'Why do they get away with it? Why let people off the hook?' There is an appeal for justice. The people of Iraq want justice to be seen to be done when Saddam Hussein comes to the courts. Those who suffered under Slobodan Milosevic are appalled at the prospect of no justice, despite years in the courts in the Hague. We want to see evil judged. We want to see justice restored. We want to see order in our society. Perhaps that's why, in Psalm 96, the thought of the Lord coming in judgement is greeted with joy. Maybe that is the perspective in which we should see the theme of judgement. Nevertheless, judgement is not a subject we consider without other emotions too. We shouldn't read these passages without tears in our eyes.

In David Prior's commentary he mentions the story of D. L. Moody, the American evangelist, who was in Chicago holding a series of evenings presenting the truth of the gospel. On the first evening, he spoke about the reality of hell and judgement and told them to come back the following night to hear about 'God's blockade on the path to hell', the good news of the gospel. That very night there was an enormous fire in Chicago, and thousands of citizens lost their lives, including people who had been at that meeting. D. L. Moody vowed never again to preach about hell or judgement without mentioning the cross, the broken heart of God which took Jesus to Calvary. I think it's in that atmosphere that we look at the certainty of God's judgement.

The first woe: selfish ambition (verses 6–8)

Look at how it's expressed: 'Woe to him who piles up stolen goods and makes himself wealthy by extortion!' (verse 6). The Babylonians were well known for greed and injustice. They robbed other nations and accumulated more and more by trampling on others. They feathered their own nest at the expense of everybody else. It's a good description of what Habakkuk said in chapter 2:5, describing the ungodly as constantly wanting more. Most of us are familiar with that. It's really the creed of our own day – grab all you can, look after number one. People are driven to want more and more and don't mind whom they trample on in the process.

Verse 7 also describes the outcome. They may think they are invincible, these proud Babylonians. They may seem triumphant as they mock God. But do they get away with it? Is it all out of control? Look at verse 7. 'Will not your debtors suddenly arise? Will they not wake up and make you tremble? Then you will become their victim.' This is the device used throughout the taunt song. The Lord turns the tables. The plunderer, verse 8, will be plundered. A time will come when Babylon will be judged just as the Lord predicted. Daniel records it in Daniel chapter 5. Belshazzar, king of Babylon, was feasting, enjoying the fruit of all his ill-gotten gains, and the finger of God came writing on the wall. 'That very night Belshazzar, king of the Babylonians, was slain, and Darius the Mede took over the kingdom' (Dan. 5:30). It's an important reminder for Christians who wonder about the apparent success of evil in our world, who might be tempted to believe that the fat cats really will succeed. One day, God says, the plunderer will be plundered. The victor will become the victim.

What about our own attitude, even as believers? It's very easy for Christians to be caught up with the perils of unjust gain and the dangers of greed, to have our eyes on selfish ambition, personal gain, rather than living by faith in the Sovereign Lord.

The second woe: false security (verses 9–11)

Again it's another graphic description of the person or the nation who thinks they are in control. 'Woe to him who builds his realm by unjust gain to set his nest on high, to escape the clutches of ruin!' It's false security. The Babylonians captured nations around them and created buffer zones to create a measure of security. The attitude is common enough. People do everything they can to protect themselves against disaster. They think they have made it. Or have they?

The Lord again pronounces the outcome (verse 11). The stones of their buildings will be a testimony against them. Nebuchadnezzar was enormously proud of his palace complex. In the outer courts of that wall, which were some 136 feet thick, every single brick had the name 'Nebuchadnezzar' written on it. And there is considerable irony in verse 10, 'You have forfeited your life.' Nebuchadnezzar of Babylon thought he had the whole world. But 'what does it profit a man to gain the whole world and forfeit his life?' (Mk. 8:36). It's a terrible thing to get to the end of your life and discover you have missed the point. Everything is wasted. The message in Habakkuk's day and ours is plain. Judgement will come. Just as for Belshazzar, the writing is on the wall. It's a certainty.

Think again of those two alternatives that we looked at in verse 4. Our calling as the righteous is to live by faith. So where does our security lie as God's people? Margaret and I recently enjoyed going to a friend's birthday party, and the conversations there surprised both of us. For Christian and non-Christian alike, the subject of security dominated the conversation. I suppose it was because most of us were fifty-somethings confronting our mid-life crises and wondering about the future. But what kind of security? It was second homes, property, house moves, early retirement, pension provision. We can easily get sucked into the same way of thinking as this world. We can get dangerously close to the false security of trusting the things of this world instead of trusting the Lord himself.

I have a friend who works in Sierra Leone, Davidson Scott. He lived through the war in Sierra Leone and witnessed a great deal of suffering. This is what he wrote, 'The only security we have is God and the only assurance we have, that which no man can take away from us, is our salvation. I am learning to look at what matters in life, not to waste time on things that do not have eternal value.'

The third woe: ruthless power (verses 12,13,17)

'Woe to him who builds a city with bloodshed and establishes a town by crime!' (verse 12). Nebuchadnezzar's palace would certainly have impressed the tourists. But it did not impress God. He saw the blood of untold people who went into making that great edifice. Notice the chilling outcome which is declared in these verses, an echo of what Jeremiah prophesied about Babylon in Jeremiah 51, 'This is what the LORD Almighty says: "Babylon's thick wall will be levelled and her high gates set on fire; the peoples exhaust themselves for nothing, the nations' labour is only fuel for the flames."' All of that effort in self aggrandisement on the part of Nebuchadnezzar and his successors, the selfish ambition, false security and ruthless power: it all goes up in smoke. Do you remember the psalm which says, 'Unless the LORD builds the house, its builders labour in vain' (Ps. 127:1). The word the psalmist uses for 'vain' is exactly the same word used in verse 13: they are working for 'nothing'. Everything the Babylonians have done will be fuel for the fire of God's judgement.

Ultimately, if you live your life without trusting God, it will all be reduced to ashes. How can you be so certain about that? See verse 13, 'Has not the LORD Almighty determined [it]' the Yahweh of hosts, the warrior God, the one who will come in salvation and judgement?

It reminds us of Paul in 1 Corinthians where he talks about the question, 'How are you building?' What kind of building are you constructing? As believers our lives are secure on that one foundation of Jesus Christ but, Paul says, what materials are you using as you build on that foundation? Are you using those things which are of passing value – 'wood, hay and stubble'? Or are you using something that will last for ever – 'gold, silver and precious stones'? How you live your life now matters because, one day, it will be tested. That's not to cast doubt on our future hope; it is simply to underline that the way in which we live our lives does make a difference. Will we look back on our lives and see that we have built with only things which are temporary, or will we have used our time, gifts and talents to have built something that will last for eternity? Will it disappear in a cloud of smoke because it has all been selfish ambition, or will it be lasting, built for eternity?

Notice that each 'woe' that we have looked at so far implies that there is something inbuilt about ungodly behaviour, as it sows the seeds of its own destruction. In a recent article entitled 'Are you sinning comfortably?', the social commentator Brian Appleyard tried to update the seven deadly sins. What interested me were his conclusions about justice and judgement. He said

> The secular minded will shrug their shoulders: it is their favourite gesture. 'So what?' they will say. There is no God to punish us and no hell in which we shall burn. And, unless taken to extremes, none of these sins in themselves is actually criminal. But the point about the 'deadlies' is they're usually their own punishment.

There is something built into them which ultimately destroys the person. God is not mocked: we reap what we sow.

For Habakkuk, it was not simply the inevitable law of retribution. Judgement is certain because of the reality of God. It is his world, it's under his control. His judgements will set things right.

The fourth woe: shameless exploitation (verses 15–17)

There are a couple of things in these verses to mention. Verse 17 first: 'The violence you have done to Lebanon will overwhelm you, and your destruction of animals will terrify you.' It's interesting that the Lord does not miss one of the elements of exploitation of which the Babylonians were guilty: the exploitation of creation, the terrible environmental damage that resulted from Babylonian invasion. We should not miss God's concern about the devastation to his creation. People these days talk about 'green theology', and we should not imagine that it is of just marginal interest. God is concerned about the impact of sin in every corner of his creation, including the destruction of forests and cruelty to animals, both of which are mentioned in verse 17. Again the outcome is announced: 'The violence you have done ... will overwhelm you' (verse 17).

The other element of exploitation which resonates with us is found in verses 15 and 16. We identify with this in our culture. 'Woe to him who gives drink to his neighbours, pouring it from the wineskin till they are drunk, so that he can gaze on their naked bodies.' This is directed at those who use alcohol to seduce people, something brought to prominence in our day through trials of date rape. But I think the point of this woe is broader than that. The ungodly have very little respect for the dignity of other people. They will go to any means to achieve their purpose. Other people are simply objects, manipulated and exploited in any way that is necessary. It is glorying in power over others. Whether that is the exploitation of cheap Chinese labourers, or Albanian and Russian women in the western European brothels, or the exploitation of children in sweatshops, or hostages in Iraq, or the trafficking of refugees – all of these are graphic illustrations of what happens when people live their lives without God.

Notice the same pattern in this woe as all the others. He has brought shame on others (verse 15). Now the Lord will bring shame on him. Look at those chilling words: 'Now it is your turn! Drink and be exposed! The cup from the LORD's right hand is coming ... and disgrace will cover your glory' (verse 16).

Imagine Belshazzar back at the feast. Right at the beginning of Daniel chapter 5 they are feasting and drinking – the Babylonians were renowned for their drunkenness. And they were drinking from the goblets from the Temple. Belshazzar gave orders to bring in the gold and silver goblets that Nebuchadnezzar had taken from the Temple in Jerusalem. And as they drank their wine, and praised their gods, the hand of the Sovereign Lord appeared and wrote. Habakkuk 2:16 was fulfilled. 'Now it's your turn! Drink ... the cup from the LORD's right hand is coming'.

God sees what is happening and God acts. The cup of judgement will come. The image is used by various Old Testament prophets: Jeremiah – 'the cup filled with the wine of my wrath'; Ezekiel – 'a cup large and deep, it will bring scorn and derision'.

It takes us to Gethsemane. Jesus, who knew all of these Old Testament passages, takes from his Father the cup of judgement. It's no wonder that initially he shrank from taking it. The cup represented God's judgement which our sins deserved, but which Jesus was to face at the cross. Jesus drank that cup to the dregs: he bore our sin, took our judgement and his drinking of that cup means that we will never hear God's 'woe' to us. The righteous live by faith in what Jesus has done on the cross in taking that cup of God's judgement. For all true believers, Paul's confident assertion should be written across the woes of Habakkuk chapter 2: 'there is now no condemnation for those for who are in Christ Jesus' (Rom. 8:1).

The fifth woe: foolish idolatry (verses 18–20)

In many ways, this is the culmination of them all. We have looked at the two alternatives to life, and here is the most obvious example of life lived without the true God: it is the folly of the worship of dumb idols. The Babylonians often ascribed their success to their gods. They looked for guidance from the idols of their own making. There is a fair amount of satirical mockery in verses 18 and 19, as elsewhere in the Old Testament, and its purpose is to demonstrate the difference between the powerless non-entities of the pagan nations and Israel's living all-powerful, all-controlling God. These verses highlight the folly of trusting in something of my own making. '… he who makes it trusts in his own creation; he makes idols that cannot speak. … Can it give guidance?' (verses 18, 19).

We may think this is pagan religion, distant from contemporary western culture, but it is very typical of our society as well. People are longing for guidance, for those things that would make sense of their lives, that give them some sense of control. So they turn to astrology or ouija boards, or to New Age or superstition. G.K. Chesterton was quite right when he said, 'When people stop believing in the truth, they don't believe in nothing, they believe in anything.' Contemporary idolatry is all around us.

Men and women of every age and culture seek substitute deities. Perhaps most obviously in our culture, the main idol is the self. Brian Appleyard, in the article I mentioned a moment ago, says: 'The only possible sin today is the sin against oneself.' The idea is everywhere. Self-help, self-esteem, making the best of oneself, looking one's best, self-realisation: we have become the centre of our little universe.

Do you know the joke, 'what's the difference between God and a lawyer'? Answer: God doesn't think he's a lawyer. But we shouldn't be too tough on the lawyers: the attitude is true of us all. We think we're in charge. And whatever the substitute god – possessions, plans, self-obsession – God pronounces his woe on all who trust in things of their own creation. Notice verse 18, 'Of what value is an idol, since a man has carved it? Or an image that teaches lies?' It's an intriguing suggestion, an idol that lies. It is counterfeit. The idols in people's lives are self-deceiving, they blind people to their own helplessness. They deceive them about their guilt and their need of forgiveness. They are ignorant of the fact that they depend on God himself for every breath they take.

The Lord is never unable to see, hear, speak or act. He is the Lord of heaven and earth. And so let's come to the final certainty.

The certainty of God's rule

I want us to finish by focusing on two wonderful certainties, one present and one future.

A present reality (verse 20)

Notice the context (verse 19). The idols are dumb – silent. But now the word comes, 'the LORD is in his holy temple let [the world] be silent before him' (verse 19). It is onomatopoeic in Hebrew, like our word 'Hush!'. Be silent, stop all the arguments, all the arrogant assertions of human power, the efforts of human glory, the petty ambitions. It's a call for reverence, because here is the Lord of the universe. He is the

Sovereign Lord, active in history; he calls all men and women, all nations, all governments to bow the knee to him.

Verse 20 represents the answer to Habakkuk's complaint. Why isn't God acting in the way Habakkuk thought he should? The Lord is seated on his kingly throne, in the place of ultimate authority, above heaven and earth, high above his creatures. Before him there is no room for asserting our independence. Instead, we are called to humble submission to the Lord of the universe. And unlike the fickle deities of paganism, here is the God who is in control, who can be relied upon. Here is the unchanging Ruler of the universe, a universe which he created and sustains and which ultimately he will wrap up and bring to completion. We don't need images, idols, magic or black arts. People didn't in Habakkuk's day either. They were called into relationship with the Sovereign Lord.

A future certainty (verse 14)

'For the earth will be filled with knowledge of the glory of the LORD, as the waters cover the sea' (verse 14). It's an incredible shaft of light in the darkness. In the context of the power of empires and the pretensions of human rulers, the Lord speaks of the certainty of what will be left in that final day: the universal knowledge of the glory of God. Similar words are used by Isaiah too: 'They will neither harm nor destroy on all my holy mountain, for the earth will be full of the knowledge of the LORD as the waters cover the sea' (Is. 11:9) He looks at that great Messianic era, which pointed to Jesus himself, the One who ultimately would bring the victory of God's purposes, the destruction of evil, the salvation of his people and the establishment of a new heaven and a new earth.

Habakkuk adds one extra word to Isaiah's phrase: the word 'glory'. 'For the earth will be filled with the knowledge *of the glory* of the LORD, as the waters cover the sea' (Hab. 2:14). Perhaps it's because 'glory' encompasses the ultimate goal of all human history – the glory of God.

If we are uncertain about what is happening in our world, this is where everything is heading. All other glories will fade away in the light of that ultimate glory, his royal majesty. Verse 14 is a wonderful description of the ultimate triumph of God. 'Jesus shall reign where'er the sun does his successive journeys run. His kingdoms stretch from shore to shore till moons shall wax and wane no more.' This is not only a great encouragement to Christians who wonder 'Where is this world heading?', but it is a great incentive to us in the task of telling others the good news of the gospel. As Psalm 96 encourages us, 'Declare his glory among the nations'. That's an act of worship as we declare God's glory. And that's an act of mission, as we declare his glory among the nations. God's people are motivated by God's glory. We know where it is heading, as verse 14 declares. Ultimately, every knee will bow to Jesus Christ.

David Bryant defines a world Christian in this way

> A world Christian is someone who is so gripped by the glory of God and the glory of his global purpose, that he chooses to align himself with God's mission to fill the earth with the knowledge of his glory as the waters cover the sea. The burning prayer of the world Christian is, 'Let the peoples praise thee O God, let all the peoples praise thee (Ps. 96:3).

The last word will not be earth's kingdoms. Habakkuk gives us a very different perspective of who's in control. It will be a glorious world filled with the awareness of God's purposes, of God's presence, and of God's glory.

On the Sunday after 9/11 in our church in Oxford, we sang a wonderful hymn, 'All my hope on God is founded' and it has a very appropriate verse after 9/11. 'Pride of man and earthly glory, sword and crown betray his trust; with what care and toil he buildeth, tower and temple fall to dust. But God's power, hour by hour, is my temple and my tower.' This verse, Habakkuk 2:14, is the very reason Habakkuk could go on trusting God in a world of darkness and uncertainty. And so can we, because the reality of verse 14 has already been achieved through the work of Jesus Christ. All our hope on God is founded.

Let's remind ourselves of these two great certainties: God's judgement and the absolute certainty of God's glorious rule. The man or woman of faith lives in submission to the Lord who is in his holy Temple. We live our lives now in the light of the truth about Jesus Christ which Paul proclaimed

> Therefore God exalted him to the highest place and gave him the name which is above every name, that at the name of Jesus every knee should bow, in heaven and on earth and under the earth, and every tongue confess that Jesus Christ is Lord, to the glory of God the Father.

And all of God's people said, 'Amen'!

Watch!

Habakkuk 3:1–16

Some years ago I had my first and only experience of abseiling, a sport that involves being dropped over a cliff backwards. You are roped up and then the person at the top belays the rope, letting you down at the speed of your choosing. You have to trust the rope but you also need to trust the person at the top. He was a good friend and I knew he wouldn't let me down! As in so many situations of life, trust grows out of our knowledge of the person.

The story of Habakkuk has confronted us with that one major question: can we trust God's purposes for our life, our future, our nation, our universe? Ultimately it all depends on our view of God. In the 1960s, the American writer, A. W. Tozer, called the evangelical church to face the critical need of revival in the face of decline. How could this be achieved? Tozer wrote

> The answer might easily disappoint some persons, for it is anything but profound. I bring no esoteric cryptogram, no mystic code to be

painfully deciphered, I appeal to no hidden law of the unconscious, no occult knowledge meant only for the few. The secret is an open one which the wayfaring man may read. It is simply the old and ever-new counsel: Acquaint thyself with God. To regain her lost power the church must see heaven opened and have a transforming vision of God.

As we open Habakkuk chapter 3, we have that opportunity.

How can we possibly understand the infinite, majestic God? St Augustine was walking along the seashore, reflecting on the question of the majesty of God, when he saw a small boy. The boy had dug a hole in the sand. He had a large shell and he ran down to the sea, filling the shell with seawater, and then returned and poured the seawater into the hole. Augustine asked him what was he doing and the boy said, 'I'm going to pour the sea into that hole.' At that point, Augustine realised what he had been trying to do: standing at the ocean of God's greatness and trying to grasp it with his finite mind. It's an almost overwhelming idea, to attempt to understand the manifestation of God's greatness and glory.

We long for a deeper understanding and experience of God. We are hungry for that reality. Don Carson has expressed it like this

> The one thing we most urgently need in Western Christendom is a deeper knowledge of God. We need to know God better. When it comes to knowing God we are a culture of the spiritually stunted. So much of our religion is packaged to address our felt needs – and these are almost uniformly anchored in our pursuit of our own happiness and fulfilment. We are not captivated by his holiness and love; his thoughts and words capture too little of our imagination, too little of our discourse, too few of our priorities.

Habakkuk's journey is nearly over. But before his closing doxology he is called to open his eyes to a remarkable, transforming vision of God. It is a vision of who God is, and a vision of his actions, past, present and future. It is a call to watch!

1. Habakkuk's appeal (verses 1,2)

Verse 1 is introduced as a prayer. Actually, it's a song. There are several clues, particularly in the musical terms. *Selah*, as far as we know, is a musical break (verses 3,9,13). Right at the end, there is a musical instruction (verse 19). In verse 1 there is a rather unusual word, *shigionoth*, probably an instruction about tempo, implying a fairly strong rhythm. This wasn't some funeral chant. Given the content of this particular song, with its dynamic elements, it was up-tempo. When I read it, I can hear the brass section, the drums, the driving rhythm of the bass. So after all we have looked at, all the struggles, challenges and turmoil for Habakkuk, he starts singing. And he encourages other people to start singing too.

One way in which God's people keep going when they are facing challenges of all kinds is to sing about what God has done. I meet it in country after country. It is fantastic to see God's people, despite the pressures, some in very small minorities, caught up in singing about what God has done. We do that because singing captures our hearts and our emotions as well as our minds. That's why the longest book in the Bible is the Psalms, a songbook.

The whole chapter represents one of the model prayers from which we can learn so much. Let's look at three things about Habakkuk's appeal.

a) A conviction about God's work (verse 2)

'LORD, I have heard of your fame; I stand in awe of your deeds, (*verse* 2) O LORD' (verse 2). Notice the change of tone from the way in which he was praying in chapter 1. Here there is a sense of humble commitment. He is no longer arguing, for he recognises that everything that God has said and done is just. Calvin translates the verse 'I heard thy voice'. Standing there on the walls above Jerusalem, Habakkuk had heard God's word, the report of God's work, both in the past and in the prophecies of what was to come. He stands in awe, alarmed almost, with a sense of submission and godly fear. Habakkuk has recognised that God is in control of the situation and so, right at the beginning of his prayer, he is accepting the just purposes of God. 'Yes Lord, now I understand.'

b) A call for God's action (verse 2)

'Renew them in our day, in our time make them known' (verse 2). Secondly, Habakkuk longs that God's powerful work in the past should be seen in his own day, for the people of God to know that he is in control of their lives and of history. Chapter 3 has many references to the story of the Exodus – their finest hour. And so he appeals 'Please Lord, repeat that kind of redemption. Renew your work now just as you did in the past.' It's a call for God's action.

As I prepared these verses, I couldn't help thinking about what dominates my praying. Is this the kind of prayer that I pray? Are we longing for God's purposes to be fulfilled? For the church to be renewed? One of the great challenges is the fact that we live in a continent where, by and large, the church is not growing. The majority of God's people today are found in the southern hemisphere. The reason for the shift in the centre of gravity is the extraordinary passion and prayerfulness of God's people in some of those countries. I have a friend who is a Langham scholar and he wondered if there was some relation between the suffering, pressure, poverty and challenge of living in some of these majority world countries, and the extraordinary sense of dependence of God's people and the blessing which he brings. There's a correlation between those things: dependent prayer and God's blessing.

When he says, 'in our day', perhaps he is meaning 'even in the midst of judgement, Lord, come in deliverance.' Although we will stress the importance of calling to mind what God has done in the past, Habakkuk is not meaning that our experience is just hearsay or second-hand. Rather, he appeals that they would experience God's saving presence just as they did in the past.

c) A cry for God's mercy (verse 2)

You can hear his aching heart in the third element of his prayer, expressed in verse 2: 'in wrath remember mercy'. It's an understandable cry. He had heard of God's judgement on his own people in Judah, the fearful reality of God's anger against sin, and so he prays that, alongside God's wrath, he would remember mercy. Once again, his prayer is a model to us. The essence of prayer is 'to plead God's character in God's presence'. 'Remember mercy, Lord, be true to your character.'

You may have noticed several references in this chapter to God's wrath. Some of the words are quite uncomfortable. His raging wrath is his hot anger, and some Christians today hesitate to ascribe such emotions to God. Isn't wrath a figment of the imagination of frustrated preachers who like to adopt the role of an austere prophet? We might be disturbed to discover that, in the Old Testament alone, there are over twenty words for God's wrath and anger, and over five hundred and eighty references to him acting in that way.

If we stand back for a moment, we can see why his wrath is essential to our understanding of God. How can God be God, if he does not reveal his wrath against all ungodliness? Paradoxically, it's because of God's wrath against wickedness that we have the comfort of knowing that his justice will be fulfilled, that the day of restoration will finally come.

In Mark Meynell's book on the cross, he quotes the true story of the nail bombings which occurred in London some years ago. The nail bomber was targeting particular minority groups: one bomb went off in Brixton, one in Brick Lane, and then a third bomb went off in a gay pub in Soho. A day later a young man was captured by the police. His name was David Copeland and he was charged with the bombings. His father, Stephen, made a press statement in which he said that he and his family totally condemned the barbaric bombings. 'If David is guilty of these awful acts of violence then we also totally condemn him for carrying out those acts.' To condemn their son did not deny their love for him, nor would the call for crimes to be punished. The call for wrongs to be righted can co-exist with deep love and compassion.

I am not the only one who identifies with Habakkuk's cry, 'Lord, in wrath remember mercy.' I saw a cartoon not long ago, with a husband and a wife standing in a queue before the gates of heaven. Waiting for their turn to face judgement, the wife whispered to her husband, 'Now, Harold, whatever you do, please don't demand what's coming to you.' We know what we deserve. But wrath and mercy are found together right at the heart of the Christian gospel, there at the cross, and it is important to hold these truths together.

These days people tend to polarise. It's not unusual to say: 'Let's emphasis God's love. Let's play down the idea of God's wrath.' But these two things always belong together. The Bible frequently describes this duality within God. If you want a very good book on the whole subject, then John Stott's book, *The Cross of Christ*, explains this duality. Remember Exodus 34, where God is described as 'the compassionate and gracious God ... Yet he does not leave the guilty unpunished'. Or Isaiah 45, 'A righteous God and a Saviour'. Paul reminds us of the 'kindness and the severity of God'. In the same way, we see that his wrath and love belong together. We have to take into our thinking not some innocuous compromise but two dynamic concepts which are complementary in God's nature and his actions.

We know how important it is to take the words of Habakkuk's prayer, and to appeal for God's mercy on the grounds of Christ's work. Whatever Habakkuk teaches us about the inevitability of judgement and God's wrath, it also points us to the Lord who shows mercy, the Lord who will redeem his people.

Here, then, are three elements to shape our prayers: a conviction about God's work, a call for God's action and a cry for God's mercy.

2. Habakkuk's vision (verses 3–15)

These verses introduce a profound revelation of God's nature and work. They remind us of the story of Job, who confronted similar challenges to Habakkuk and asked similar questions. But although Job asks 'Why?', God answers: 'Who?' God's reply is not a detailed argument but an extraordinary panorama of his power and wisdom. Job is not given neat solutions and neither is Habakkuk, but rather he is given an overwhelming vision of God.

God comes to individuals in a whole variety of unexpected ways: a burning bush; a ladder of angels; a still, small voice; a wheel in a wheel; a lofty throne; a solar eclipse; a sheet filled with animals; a trumpet sound. Each announces the coming of the Lord. That's what Habakkuk discovers here. The vision swept him off his feet. He was sent reeling by the remarkable vision of the warrior God outlined in these verses. His reactions are described either side of the vision. Verse 2: 'I have heard of your fame; I stand in awe of your deeds'. Verse 16: 'I heard and my heart pounded, my lips quivered at the sound; decay crept into my bones, and my legs trembled.'

The vision has a number of important references to what God has done in the past. He retraces the route taken by the Israelites in the Exodus, when God delivered his people. Remembering God's acts in the past is basic to Old Testament prayer, and very important for us Christians. When we are bewildered about our own world, we are called to remember what God has done in the past. But as Martin Luther expressed it, 'there is nothing so short as the believer's memory.'

In the Old Testament, the call to remember is very common. Recalling what God had done in the past was an incentive to live life now with more wholehearted trust. They were encouraged to keep rehearsing the stories of the great saving events in their history. Why? They were reminders of God's grace. They reinforced the reality of God's love for his people. If you asked God's people in the Old Testament, 'How do you know God loves you?', their reply would be, 'Look at what God has done for us. He rescued us from Egypt, he cared for us in the wilderness, and he defeated our enemies.' These were the great historical realities on which their faith was founded.

When we are tempted to think that God must have forgotten about us, as Habakkuk did, or God doesn't really care, then we look at the cross and the resurrection. Our faith is not founded on nice religious ideas. It is founded on what Jesus has done.

The vision in Habakkuk 3 includes these backward glances, but Habakkuk also looks at the present in the light of the future. We find a kaleidoscope of references, sometimes looking back and sometimes forward. Let's highlight three features of the vision.

a) The coming of the Lord (verses 3–5)

The vision begins by proclaiming that God is on the move. As he comes nearer and nearer, the impact of his glorious presence becomes more and more dramatic. 'God came from Teman, the Holy One from Mount Paran' (verse 3). This is a reference to the area of Sinai, where

God first revealed himself to Moses at the burning bush, and subsequently, in a dramatic revelation of his power and presence, revealed the law to his people. Verses 3 and 4 describe the radiance of his presence as he comes. 'His glory covered the heavens and his praise filled the earth. His splendour was like the sunrise; rays flashed from his hand, where his power was hidden.'

The verses conjure up the fire and cloud of that Mount Sinai encounter, reminding Habakkuk, and all singers of this song, of the glory and power of God whenever he comes to his people. Just as at Sinai, his coming is accompanied by a radiance that is overwhelming and awe-inspiring. Habakkuk sees it here illuminating the entire world.

In *The Message*, Eugene Peterson paraphrases it like this, 'Skies are blazing with his splendour, his praises sounding through the earth. His cloud-brightness like dawn, exploding, spreading, forked-lightning shooting from his hand – what power hidden in that fist!' That's the drama and the colour of this remarkable vision of the coming of God. In his coming in the Exodus, he was accompanied by extraordinary signs, described in verse 5: 'Plague went before him; pestilence followed his steps.' The Egyptians, powerful though they were, were terrified by that coming of the Lord.

Habakkuk remembers those great events of the past but, as throughout the song, there is an anticipation of God's future intervention. God's coming will always be a source of hope for God's people. As we saw from Hebrews 10, the writer quotes from Habakkuk chapter 2 verse 3, making application to the coming of the Lord. 'do not throw away your confidence; it will be richly rewarded. You need to persevere … For in just a very little while' (here he quotes Habakkuk) 'He who is coming will come and will not delay' (Heb. 10: 35–37).

The glorious manifestation of God's coming described in Habakkuk 3 verses 3 and 4, winessed by the entire universe, also anticipates that day when we will see Jesus coming. Matthew describes the similar dramatic manifestations accompanying that arrival: 'For as lightning that comes from the east is visible even in the west, so will be the coming of the Son of Man ... They will see the Son

of Man coming on the clouds of the sky, with power and great glory'
(Mt. 24:27,30).

This is where Habakkuk's vision is pointing us: to that ultimate
day. God declares, 'Watch, I am coming. This coming will be a day of
judgement and of deliverance, a day of wrath and of mercy.' And
when he comes, human history will be finally wrapped up. So we are
called to watch, to look for 'the glorious appearing of our great God
and Saviour, Jesus Christ'.

Lord Shaftesbury, the great social reformer who was totally
committed to the needs of this world, also had another horizon. Near
the end of his life he said, 'I do not think that in the last forty years I
have lived one conscious hour that was not influenced by the thought
of the Lord's return.'

b) The power of the Lord (verses 6,7)

Just as there were great convulsions at Sinai when God came to his
people, so his power is demonstrated whenever he comes in salvation and deliverance. The poetry of verse 6 demonstrates the cosmic
implications of his arrival: 'He stood, and shook the earth; he looked
and made the nations tremble. The ancient mountains crumbled and
the age-old hills collapsed.' He is the Creator and at his coming even
the mountains crumble before him. The eternal hills bow before the
splendour of this eternal God. Cushan and Midian (verse 7) were
nations which bordered Egypt, so they would have seen the great
deliverance that God brought about for his people, and trembled
with distress and anguish (verse 7). No nation would be exempt from
his power and his judgement.

Isaiah uses exactly the same language. Writing to those in his own
day who were tempted to believe that God had given up on his
people, Isaiah says, 'Who has measured the waters in the hollow of
his hand … Who has held the dust of the earth in a basket, or weighed
the mountains on the scales … He sits enthroned above the circle of
the earth, and its people are like grasshoppers' (Is. 40:12,22). The
early Christians began their prayer in Acts 4: 'Sovereign Lord, you
made the heaven and the earth'. Their appeal was based on the fact
that the powerful Lord of creation was in control of the forces ranged

against them. The centre of power today is not London, Washington, or Moscow: it is the Lord God Omnipotent.

Many of the descriptive images in Habakkuk 3 are picked up in the New Testament. Peter describes the cataclysmic events of the end times: 'The heavens will disappear with a roar; the elements will be destroyed by fire, and the earth and everything in it will be laid bare. ... That day will bring about the destruction of the heavens by fire, and the elements will melt in the heat. But in keeping with his promise, we are looking forward to a new heaven and a new earth, the home of righteousness' (2 Pet. 3:10,12,13). Peter is making it abundantly clear to the people of his day, just as Habakkuk did, that this *will* happen. God is in control of this world.

In David Atkinson's commentary on the book of Job, he recounts the story of a pastor, making his way back home during the Second World War, after a night of comforting people in the London blitz. He meets a fellow pastor who had been doing the same thing, but who was bewildered and exasperated as he sought to care for broken people. He explained, 'I wish I was on the throne of the universe for just ten minutes.' His colleague, who wasn't quite so far gone, replied, 'If you were on the throne for ten minutes I would not wish to live in your universe for ten seconds.' That's the reality. In chapter 3 Habakkuk is describing the powerful Lord of the universe, the One who is eternal and who is in control.

c) The victory of the Lord (verses 8–15)

This final section introduces a number of images associated with the Red Sea deliverance. In the dramatic poetry of the song, the Lord uses the elements of his creation in his judgement. Look at verse 8, 'Were you angry with the rivers, O LORD? Was your wrath against the streams? Did you rage against the sea when you rode with your horses and your victorious chariots?' No, he wasn't angry with them. God demonstrated his power in these elements; he was a general leading his forces. You can't miss the force of the descriptions, as he tramples the enemy under his feet (verse 12), crushing the head of the wicked (verse 13), and destroying the enemy (verse 14). There is a further allusion to the Red Sea deliverance in verse 14, demonstrating God's power even over the fearsome chaos of the sea.

The battle is fought for one clear purpose. Although there are descriptions of judgement, there are significant references to salvation. Notice in verse 8, God is riding upon his chariot of victory. The word used for 'victory' is actually 'salvation'. The Greek version of the Old Testament renders it: 'Your chariot which is salvation'. It is God coming to save.

Remember Habakkuk's first prayer: 'How long … must I call for help, but you do not listen?' (Hab. 1:2). Here in Habakkuk's vision is the proof that God hears, and that God acts. It's an account of God's deliverance of his people. It was the very thing that Habakkuk was crying out for, the assurance he needed that God keeps his promises. He remembers his covenant.

The purpose of God's coming is the salvation of his people. And that is reinforced in verse 13: 'You came out to deliver your people, to save your anointed one.' What God did in the Exodus deliverance, he will do again. He will rescue his people and he will bring them back. That happened for some of God's people after the immediate judgement that Habakkuk and Jeremiah were talking about. After the exile they finally returned home. God delivered his people, bringing them back to Jerusalem. That's one level of understanding.

These verses also anticipate the deliverance of God's people in the future as well. Notice that reference, verse 13, 'to save your anointed one.' The anointed is the Messiah, translated in the Greek as 'Christ'. The word 'anointed' was sometimes used of the kings of Israel, even of a pagan king, Cyrus, who was used by God to deliver his people. But the word also points to the final Messiah, Jesus, the Christ. At the cross, the Lord Jesus was our substitute in bearing God's righteous anger. It was there that wrath and mercy met. God raised Jesus to life – or to use the language of verse 13 – 'saved his anointed'. So Jesus won the decisive battle over human sin, over all of the cosmic hosts of wickedness.

Paul uses graphic language when he talks about Christ's victory in Colossians 2:15. 'And having disarmed the powers and authorities, he made a public spectacle of them, triumphing over them by the cross.' Many Christians and non-Christians are all too aware of the reality of evil, the reality of dark forces. Jesus' ministry was to liberate people from Satan's oppression, to liberate us from the kingdom of darkness. John summed up the purpose of Jesus' mission in 1 John 3:8, 'The reason the Son of God appeared was to destroy the devil's work', and the language of Habakkuk 3 describes the victory of the Lord, crushing the leader of the land of wickedness. '… you stripped him from head to foot' (verse 13): that immediately takes my mind to Colossians 2. '… having disarmed the powers and authorities, he made a public spectacle of them, triumphing over them by the cross' (Col. 2:15). The NIV uses the picture of evil spirit powers, terrorists from hell being stripped of their weapons. So the cross was the place of the unmasking, the disarming of every power which stands against God and against his people. Now through his death and resurrection he has freed us from the fear of evil and delivered us from every demonic force.

Habakkuk's vision, then, portrays these three realities: the coming of the Lord, the power of the Lord and and the victory of the Lord. And they point to that ultimate reality of Jesus' own victory.

Often there is a point of tension between what we believe and what's going on in our world. All I have just said about the victory of Christ on the cross, and the overcoming of every cosmic power of evil, will evoke the response that such theology doesn't match with our experience. And it's true. Satan *has* been defeated, but not been finally eliminated. We live our lives in the overlap between now and not yet, with the point of tension to which we have referred earlier. We live in a world where the influence of evil is still very evident.

I find it helpful to think of this particular illustration. Imagine that you are watching a football game, say, between Oxford United and Everton, and Oxford United scrape by, 5–1. Your team wins! A week later you are watching the video replay but, as you watch, you see Everton move forward. They're very, very fast, moving out to the wings, and you begin to wonder – they might win this game! But then you think, no, the game's already won. You know the outcome.

We Christians know the outcome. In our struggles we still face the hostility of evil, still feel the pull of sin, still know something of the evils of death. But we can be absolutely sure that Jesus has secured the victory. This is a vital perspective in our own Christian walk.

In Habakkuk's day there were all kinds of reasons to be tempted to think that God's people were losing ground, evil was triumphing, that they wouldn't finally make it. And there are all kinds of reasons why we Christians also feel much the same: perhaps we will not finally make it to our home in heaven? So we must remember this truth: the events of Christ's death and resurrection have already taken place. The outcome is already sure. Habakkuk knew, as he reeled at the overwhelming vision, that this God could be trusted with his life, with his future, and even with the destiny of the international powers. God was in control.

Looking back to the victory of the cross, looking forward to its ultimate fulfilment in the coming of Jesus Christ, let's live our lives now fully and freely in the service of Christ our Redeemer.

Worship!

Habakkuk 3:16–19

I don't think it has yet reached our shores from North America, but it is now possible to watch interactive movies. Instead of sitting back on the couch and passively watching your favourite film, you are given a remote control and, as the film proceeds, at various points the audience is invited to vote as to which way the plotline will go. So you can decide, for example, whether or not the bad guy gets caught, whether or not the couple will declare their love for each other, or whether it's the maid or the elderly uncle who commits the murder. What they have discovered is a well-known fact about human nature: people like happy endings. We love movies that have the 'happily-ever-after' feel to them.

Here we are at the end of the story of Habakkuk. Would you say it's a happy ending? In some senses, yes. There is a note of rejoicing here in these final verses which is hard to miss. But in reality the situation is as bad as ever.

It would a wrong use of language to call this a happy ending, because the situation in which Habakkuk finds himself is as terrifying as it always was. But something has happened to this man along the journey. The song in the closing verses of chapter 3 represents his final response to the overwhelming revelation of God's greatness. It has been a journey from the 'Why?' of chapter 1, now to 'Worship!' at the close of the book.

Habakkuk bows the knee to the Sovereign Lord and, in some of the most moving words in the whole Bible, he shows us the elements of true worship, the key features of living a life of faith in this uncertain world. So I have chosen four headings to summarise the song.

1. Respect for the Lord (verse 16)

If the book of Habakkuk is taught in our churches, then usually it is the closing doxology that is selected! Even those who do preach these verses often begin with verse 17. But verse 16 is an integral part of Habakkuk's response. As we saw yesterday, the vision of God's glory in chapter 3 is set within a framework. The two brackets are verses 2 and 16, both saying similar things. Chapter 3 verse 2: 'LORD, I have heard of your fame; I stand in awe of your deeds, O LORD.' He was overwhelmed as he heard the report of God's word. Then verse 16, 'I heard and my heart pounded, my lips quivered at the sound; decay crept into my bones, and my legs trembled.'

Having encountered God's majesty and power, having seen God's judgement, he was shaken to the core of his being. Verse 16 describes how he was near to collapse. He trembled like a leaf. He shook from head to toe. He was speechless. Habakkuk records that he felt the impact of this encounter, not simply hearing God's word but now experiencing him. He had questioned God in the past about his character, his work and his righteousness. He had appealed for evidence of God's power and of God's control in this uncertain world of his. And now he had heard, now he had seen the vision, the revelation from the Lord. He could barely stand up. He was profoundly shaken with a sense of awe, a deep respect for the Lord.

He had got the message. Habakkuk and the people were not going to escape the reality of God's discipline, expressed in the judgement he was going to bring through the Babylonians. It would soon be upon them. We will see exactly what that discipline meant when we come to verse 17. But I am sure that for Habakkuk it wasn't simply a reaction of fear, as he thought about the judgement which was to come, though doubtless that was part of his reaction. It must also have been a response to the extraordinary revelation of God's character that he had just experienced in the vision of chapter 3.

There are many examples in the Bible of a similar reaction on the part of those who came into God's presence. Job's response to the encounter with the living God was: 'I am unworthy.' Like Habakkuk, he was speechless in the face of what God had said and done. Or Isaiah, seeing the throne in Isaiah 6. What was his response? He wasn't proud that God had enabled him to see the greatness and the holiness of God. It was quite the reverse. 'Woe to me!' I cried. 'I am ruined! For I am a man of unclean lips'.

Every so often in the Gospels there were glimpses of Jesus' own glory and power. For example, following that incredible fishing expedition, Peter finally said, 'Go away from me, LORD; I am a sinful man!' Or John, in Revelation 1, seeing the ascended Christ amongst the lampstands: what was his response? 'When I saw him, I fell at his feet as though dead.'

There is an interesting book called *The Trivialisation of God*, written by Donald McCullough, and he writes this

> Unaccustomed as we are to mystery, we expect nothing even similar to Abraham's falling on his face, Moses' hiding in terror, Isaiah's crying out 'Woe is me', or Saul being knocked flat ... Reverence and awe have often been replaced by a yawn of familiarity. The consuming fire has been domesticated into a candle flame, adding a bit of religious atmosphere, perhaps, but no heat, no blinding light, no power for purification ... We prefer the illusion of a safer deity, and so we have pared God down to manageable proportions.

I am enormously grateful that in today's evangelicalism we are urged to rejoice in God's grace, to enjoy God's intimacy, and to reflect that in joyful informality. But when you read the book of Habakkuk, or some of those other passages to which I have just referred, you realise there is another side to worship, another response that is called for.

I have quoted this story before, and I hope you will forgive me if you know it, but it's a humorous example of this reality. A group of American tourists were given a tour of the Houses of Parliament. They were walking along the corridors when, coming in the opposite direction, was Lord Hailsham, then the Lord Chancellor, on his way to a civic occasion dressed in his Chancellor's robes. He saw the group of American tourists coming, but beyond them he saw the then Leader of the Opposition, Neil Kinnock. He wanted to speak to Neil Kinnock, so he lifted up his hand and said 'Neil' – and every one of the American tourists dropped to one knee. In our culture, especially in Britain, there are fewer formal expressions of reverence. But the problem is, the informality also impacts our attitude to God. As I look at the inconsistencies and the hypocrisy of my own life, and then at the fearful majesty of God which Habakkuk has been showing to us, I realise there are times when I too should tremble, when before God's majestic holiness I ought to take more than one step back. The God whom we worship, seen in this book, is the Lord God Almighty. Our worship must never lose that sense of appropriate awe. He is, as someone has said, not the All-matey, but the Almighty.

Peter Lewis, in his book, *The Living God*, says this: 'He is our Father, but he is also our holy and heavenly Father, a Father like no other, the Lord, the King. We may not stroll up to him with our hands in our pockets, whistling.' Respect for the Lord.

2. Rest in the Lord (verse 16)

'Yet I will wait paitiently for the day of calamity to come on the nation invading us' (verse 16). Here is a paradox. In verse 16 he describes how he has collapsed, trembling, and then he continues, 'Yet I will wait patiently ...' We have noticed this change of mood throughout the book. Do you remember all the restless anxiety, the questions, the perplexity of chapter 1? And now here in chapter 3: 'Yet I will wait patiently'. The situation hasn't changed. One commentator puts it, 'Nations still rage ... the arrogant still rule, the poor still suffer, the enslaved still labour for emptiness and false gods are still worshipped ...' But Habakkuk knows the One who is working his purposes out, unseen behind the turmoil.

Habakkuk knows the end. He knows that God's word is sure, that God's word can be trusted, and so he says, 'Yet I will wait patiently'. I will rest, because I know that God is true to his promises.

Spurgeon wrote a wonderful sermon on these verses. Let me quote from part of it.

> We have been assured by people who think they know a great deal about the future that awful times are coming. Be it so; it need not alarm us, for the Lord reigneth. Stay yourself on the Lord ... and you can rejoice in His name. If the worst comes to the worst, our refuge is in God; if the heavens shall fall the God of heaven will stand; when God cannot take care of His people under heaven, He will take them above the heavens and there they shall dwell with Him. Therefore, as far as you are concerned, rest; for you shall stand ... at the end of the days.

I think that captures the spirit of Habakkuk's statement. He knows that God's purposes will be fulfilled. As we saw from the vision given to Habakkuk as he stood on the watchtower, 'the revelation awaits an appointed time; it speaks of an end and will not prove false. Though it linger, *wait for it*; it will certainly come and will not delay' (Hab. 2:3). We've seen that it's a main theme in Habakkuk – how to live in the meantime, how to live in the waiting room. Not with anxiety, not with uncertainty, but resting in the sure knowledge that the God who has spoken will bring about his purposes, that the earth will be filled with the knowledge of the glory of God. 'The righteous will live by his faith.'

I hope you see that it hasn't been some cheap triumphalism. It hasn't been an easy journey for Habakkuk. He has been through all kinds of inner struggles to reach this point of rest in God. Desmond Tutu spoke these words during the struggles in South Africa: 'Sometimes you wish, of course, to say to God, "God, we know that you are in charge but why don't you make it slightly more obvious?"'

Many of us are asking that question. How was Habakkuk able to rest, to wait patiently? It was his faith in the word of God, that word of revelation. There would be discipline for God's people – he knew that was coming. And he knew that there would be exile – both he and Jeremiah prophesied it. Sure enough, the people were carted off into exile by the Babylonians. And eventually God did redeem his people, and they returned to Jerusalem. Ultimately there would also be judgement on the nation that invaded them, as verse 16 predicted. Sure enough, as we saw in the woes of chapter 2, that's exactly what happened. Nebuchadnezzar, Belshazzar and all subsequent empires have been judged by God.

Habakkuk had to look through the fog as he wondered about God's purposes, whether God really was in control. But as believers in Jesus Christ we know what God's ultimate purposes are. We hinted at them in chapter 3 as we looked at the coming of the Lord. It is expressed in the incredible mission statement that Paul gives in Ephesians 1 verse 10, when he says that God will 'bring all things in heaven and on earth together under one head, even Christ.' So the Christian church also has to walk by faith. We have to rest in God's promise, in his word, as we wait for that final deliverance.

I think we need to pause to ask if that is a reality for us? It might be easier for us to hold on in faith to the ultimate realities we have been describing: trusting God's word that Jesus will one day return, that his purposes will be fulfilled, that the earth will be filled with the knowledge of the glory of God. But we also need a practical day by day faith that keeps on trusting him and holding on to his promises.

I found it enormously helpful to read some words written by Alec Motyer on how we should pray 'Thy will be done.' At first sight you might think that that phrase 'Your will be done' imposes a restriction on our praying. But in fact, to pray 'Your will be done' lifts the restriction. Let's imagine for a moment that God was duty bound to give me everything I ask for. I think probably by tomorrow morning I would stop praying, because I have no idea what is best for me, my family, my church or my nation. It would be an intolerable burden for a limited, finite mind. So to pray 'Your will be done' lifts the restriction of my knowledge. It is to submit to the Lord God Omnipotent who knows the end from the beginning and who will bring about his good purposes. Habakkuk had learned that this is how he should live: 'Your will be done.' Despite all of the turmoil and confusion of Jerusalem, Habakkuk had learned that God could be trusted. Whatever the future, he could wait on God's purposes. Habakkuk could rest in God.

3. Rejoice in the Lord (verses 17,18)

'Yet I will rejoice in the LORD, I will be joyful in God my Saviour' (verse 18). What is so moving about this song of worship is the context in which it is sung. There is a danger that, given the familiarity and the beauty of the poetry, we miss the force of the implications of verse 17: 'Though the fig-tree does not bud and there are no grapes on the vines, though the olive crop fails and the fields produce no food, though there are no sheep in the pen and no cattle in the stalls, yet I will rejoice …'

What is Habakkuk describing in that verse? It's possible he is anticipating the ultimate Day of the Lord. But it is also highly likely that he is describing the devastating impact of the predicted coming invasion of the Babylonian war machine that we saw in chapter 1.

The verse is clear: everything has been taken away. David Prior expresses it like this: 'the ravages of war, the horrors of invasion, the devastation of nature's resources, the removal of all basic necessities'. That's what is described in verse 17. It begins with the apparent luxuries of figs, grapes, olives, but then the verse moves very quickly to show that there is no food at all. It wasn't simply a devastated economic and social infrastructure. *Everything* had gone. That's what makes this small word 'Yet' all the more remarkable. He is stripped of everything, and yet this man of faith sings 'yet I will rejoice in the

LORD'. Verse 16, '*Yet* I will wait patiently'. Verse 18, '*yet* I will rejoice'. It's Job saying, 'Though he slay me, yet will I hope in him'. It's Paul saying, 'We are hard pressed on every side, but not crushed'.

There is another famous doxology, found in Job chapter 1. Job had received the devastating news of a catalogue of disasters: his oxen, donkeys, sheep and camels had all been taken away. All of his servants had been killed. All of his children had died when the house collapsed on them. Satan's wager with God was, 'stretch out your hand and strike everything he has, and he will surely curse you to your face'. And what was Job's response? '"Naked I came from my mother's womb, and naked I depart. The LORD gave and the LORD has taken away; may the name of the LORD be praised." In all this, Job did not sin by charging God with wrongdoing' (Job 1:21,22). So instead of cursing God, Job the man of faith blessed the LORD.

Again, it's very important to see those words in their context. This is no cheap Hallelujah. Warren Wiersbe, commenting on the Job phrase says, 'Anybody can say, "The Lord gave" or "The Lord has taken away", but it takes real faith to say in the midst of sorrow and suffering, "Blessed by the name of the Lord."'

How can Habakkuk respond as he does? The key is in verse 18. What was there left for Habakkuk to rejoice in? It was not his possessions. It was certainly not his circumstances. It was not what we might call the blessings of God. None of them are there in verse 18. It was, 'rejoice *in the* LORD'. Like Job, he was stripped of everything else but God. That's the key to his joy; it is finding that God is enough. Finding that God the Creator, the Redeemer, the covenant-keeping God – he is enough. And that's how Habakkuk concludes this book. All of the things on which we rely, in our families or in our world – everything may be stripped away. But can this reality, the reality of God himself, be enough for us?

All we have seen in this book points us to this fact: for men and woman of faith, evil has lost the initiative. That's what Habakkuk came to see. God ultimately remains. When we become Christians we are not automatically beamed up into the mothership. That is not God's purpose. We are not protected from the hardships of this world. There is no guarantee for us, as God's people, that we will be immune from suffering or from God's discipline, from the oppression of enemies, from the pains and dangers of living in this broken world. But we know that the Lord will not let go of his people, that he has not abandoned his world. He is still in control. His purposes *will* be fulfilled. And since we have him, we have enough. 'Yet I will rejoice *in the* LORD, I will be joyful in God my Saviour.' Rejoicing in God alone.

It's important that I am not misunderstood here. There was a time when books were published about 'praise power'. John White calls them the 'cruel merchants of praise power' and Richard Foster wrote, 'In its worst form this teaching denies the vileness of evil and baptizes the most horrible tragedies as the will of God. Scripture commands us to live in a spirit of thanksgiving in the midst of all situations; it does not command us to celebrate the presence of evil.'

Whatever the source of the difficulty, whether satanic in origin as Job found, or simply the result of living in a fractured and fallen world, ultimately, all of these things are within the soverign purposes of God. And that's what Habakkuk came to see.

The other day I was with a group of leaders in Albania and I met a remarkable Christian from Kosovo who is now helping the small churches there. He used to run a number of businesses in Kosovo before the war, and he was very successful. He had several shops and a couple of houses, but he was also quite famous – he was a bodybuilder and eventually became the Yugoslav weightlifting champion. And, when the invasion of Kosovo came, he was forced to evacuate all of the shops. He left his home, he was beaten up, and his family was taken away as refugees. He went in search of them, and eventually he found them in Albania. Whilst he was there he came across a small Christian mission which provided food. Eventually the family returned to Kosovo. He looked for his shops, only to discover they had been completely destroyed. He looked for his two homes, but they had both been burned down. As he was walking through the city, he saw a white van with a fish on the back, and he recognised the same Christians he had met in Albania. Eventually, through their help, he came to faith in Christ. And he said to me through the translator, 'I had nothing, but I have now found everything. The Lord is my life'.

I think there would many here who could echo that sentiment. Some of you have lost partners, or lost children. Some of you have gone through all kinds of valleys. But Habakkuk's song has rung true. When everything is taken away, the Lord is my life. 'I will rejoice in God'. That is the song of the true believer. That is the song of the believing congregation, and it is confirmed because of all that Jesus has done. Rejoice in the Lord!

4. Rely on the Lord (verse 19)

Here is the fourth key to Habakkuk's worship and his life of faith. Look at verse 19, 'The Sovereign LORD is my strength; he makes my feet like the feet of a deer, he enables me to go on the heights.' In chapter 1, I mentioned that one of the important things to do when things look as though they are out of control is to remember the certainties. And that's what Habakkuk did. '*My* God, *my* Holy One, we will not die' (Hab. 1:12). And now at the end of the prophecy, in verses 18 and 19, he says exactly the same, doubtless with added vigour: 'I will be joyful in God *my* Saviour' (verse 18); 'the Sovereign LORD is *my* strength' (verse 19). He knows that he will never be separated from this Covenant God whatever is going on in the world around him. *God* is my strength. *God* is my rock.

It is precisely in these moments of pressure that we come to know the Lord in ways we would never otherwise have done. We are forced to depend on God. We trust him more than we would have done if life had been relatively straightforward.

Jim Packer, in his wonderful book *Knowing God*, has a chapter called 'These Inward Trials.'

> How does God prosecute this purpose? Not by shielding us from assault by the world, the flesh and the devil, not by protecting us from burdensome and frustrating circumstances, nor yet by shielding us from troubles created by our own temperament and psychology; but rather by exposing us to all these things, so as to overwhelm us with a sense of our own inadequacy and to drive us to cling to Him more

closely. This is the ultimate reason, from our standpoint, why God fills our lives with troubles and perplexities of one sort of another – it is to ensure that we shall learn to hold Him fast.

The Lord is my strength – the Hebrew word could also mean 'army'. The Lord is my army, the One who sustains my life, the life of the righteous who live by faith. He provides for the person who might have lost everything else, the person who has been pushed right to the limits. God the Lord is my strength, my army. He is all I need.

It's similar to the well-known testimony of Paul in 2 Corinthians 12. He had the thorn in the flesh, and how did God reply to his appeal for its removal? He said, 'My grace is sufficient for you, for my power is made perfect in weakness.' It was an unexpected answer to his prayer which became the most powerful inspiration of his life. Now God's all-sufficient grace was poured into his life, not in spite of the thorn but because of that very weakness. 'The Sovereign LORD is my strength'. The breakthrough for Paul was to see that weakness has the special advantage of making room for God's grace. It's when God can work most effectively, when his power can be most clearly seen.

It was just the same in Jeremiah's experience. He confronted a range of challenges, just like Habakkuk. He was God's opposition spokesman, against the priests, the military, the politicians. But we find some strong assurances in his call in chapter 1 verse 18. God promises that he will be 'a fortified city, an iron pillar … a bronze wall'. They are very graphic descriptions, maybe also expressing his loneliness. But God was giving him a strength that would enable him to accept his weakness and fears, and still stand up to the world.

And Habakkuk's testimony included that kind of commitment. Verse 19 implies he is now sure-footed. There is a stability and an energy. 'He enables me to go on the heights' (verse 19). So as I put my faith in him, I can live with unstumbling security, rising above all of the oppression of the world. God enables his people to keep walking, to keep climbing.

David Prior makes the legitimate point that many of us experience
spiritual vertigo. We grow queasy at the thought of some of the
spiritual challenges, the mountains we face. Our legs begin to buckle
when we think about threatening circumstances. So the result is that
we live our lives within cautiously safe limits. But God 'enables me to
go on the heights' (verse 19). Habakkuk had faced many high places,
and there were some mountains ahead too. But through his
encounter with the living God, he now knew he could rise above
those challenges because God had equipped him: 'he *enables* me'
(verse 19).

When I come to the Lake District, I nearly always think of Psalm
121, 'I lift up my eyes to the hills – where does my help come from?
My help comes from the LORD, the Maker of heaven and earth.' My
colleague, Chris Wright, heard an African preacher expound that
psalm and he preached it like this. 'I look to the hills and I think:
"However am I going to do it! It's impossible. Look at that
mountain!"' That's the opposite of how I had understood it. I see the
mountain and I think, 'How beautiful, how inspiring.' But the
African preacher thought of it quite differently. 'This mountain is
impossible, I look to the hills – where is my help going to come from?'
And so, verse 2 follows, 'My help comes from the LORD, the Maker of
heaven and earth.' He is the one who enables me to climb this
mountain. And that was Habakkuk's testimony. Whatever
mountains he faced, he could rely on the Lord.

Some commentators also remind us of one final thing: the idea of
'the heights' in verse 19. The word often refers to the high places
which were under the control of hostile forces. It might refer to
centres of pagan worship. I was in India in May and had to go over
several mountain passes. At the top you find the shrines of various
religions. Very often the high places are the places of pagan worship.
It's often symbolic, as it was in the Old Testament. The gods, they
thought, controlled the high ground, and were therefore in charge of
the whole area.

So is it possible that Habakkuk means that God enables us to go
even into those heights, those spiritual territories, those high places
of the enemy? By God's power, by God's word and by God's Spirit, he

enables us to see the gospel advance whatever the situation, whatever hostile forces may be ranged against Christ and against his people. He enables me to go on to those very heights.

There we have the four keys to his worship and his life of faith. They are: respect for the Lord, rest in the Lord, rejoice in the Lord and rely on the Lord. This has been Habakkuk's journey from the confusion of chapter 1 to the confidence of chapter 3. It's from fear to faith. It's from 'Why?' to 'Worship!' He not only saw that God was in charge of world affairs but he had come to realise it in the depth of his being. God can be trusted to do what is right. Nothing will hinder his good purposes. God has the last word. I can trust my life and my future and this universe fully to him.

My very opening words in the first exposition were to quote the title that we are looking at in Keswick, 'Out of control?' And we have seen Habakkuk's conclusion. It's not out of control. As Paul wrote

> … we know that in all things God works for the good of those who love him, who have been called according to his purpose. … Who shall separate us from the love of Christ? Shall trouble or hardship or persecution or famine or nakedness or danger or sword? As it is written: 'For your sake we face death all day long; we are considered as sheep to be slaughtered.' No, in all these things we are more than conquerors though him who loved us. For I am convinced that neither death nor life, neither angels nor demons, neither the present nor the future, nor any powers, neither height nor depth, nor anything else in all creation, will be able to separate us from the love of God that is in Christ Jesus our Lord.

The Lectures

Keswick Lecture – Week 1

When the Spirit Comes in Power

by Ian Randall

IAN RANDALL

Ian was helped in his Christian growth in the later 1960s by the Christian Union at the University of Aberdeen. He worked for several years in Personnel Management and then sensed a call to pastoral ministry. In the early 1980s he trained at Regent's Park College, Oxford, for Baptist ministry and had two Baptist pastorates. He is Deputy Principal and Lecturer in Church History and Spirituality at Spurgeon's College, London, having taught there since 1992. For three years he shared his time between Spurgeon's and the International Baptist Theological Seminary in Prague. He wrote *Transforming Keswick* with Charles Price in 2000 and has written a number of other books on evangelicalism, including *Evangelical Experiences, Educating Evangelicals, One Body in Christ* and *Spirituality and Social Change.* Ian is married to Janice, a language teacher, and they have two daughters who live in the Czech Republic.

When the Spirit Comes in Power

Introduction

I want to say thank you to the Keswick Council for the opportunity to speak on the Welsh revival of 1904–5. I felt it was rather a bold move, to ask a Scot to come and do this. Being part of the wider Celtic community is certainly part of my story and also I have been part of communities of believers who have been greatly concerned to see renewal and revival. The concern is not to go back to the past and live in the past. But we can and should go back through church history and recognise that there are warnings there for us, there are things from which we can gain wisdom, and there is much inspiration for us. It will be my purpose to bring some of this out as we share the story of the Welsh revival.

I will read two verses from Psalm 44. Verse 1 says, 'We have heard with our ears, O God; our fathers have told us what you did in their days, in days long ago.' And then, at the end of the psalm, the psalmist says, 'Rise up and help us; redeem us because of your unfailing love.' In other words, 'Those things that you have done before, those great acts of love and power, do them again.'

My own initial awareness of the Welsh revival goes back to the year 1969. A book came out, in that year, by Eifion Evans.[1] It was about the Welsh revival and it had a foreword by Dr Martyn Lloyd Jones. He saw the need for a study of revival as being opportune

---

[1]   Eifion Evans, *The Welsh Revival of 1904* (London: Evangelical Press, 1969).

because (among other things) of the charismatic movement that was emerging in the 1960s and a new interest in spiritual phenomena. Since those first days a number of books have come out. I commend to you a whole set that has come out by Kevin Adams. I am very grateful to Kevin Adams and to Crusade for World Revival for permission to use some of these as illustrations.[2]

I want to look, very briefly, at the broader context of revival, including the holiness movements which brought the Keswick Convention into being in 1875. Then I will examine what led up to revival. Then, thirdly, I want to look at the story of an amazing two years, 1904–5, in which the Welsh revival was at its height. I want to comment, especially, on the links with Keswick because this is clearly a challenge for us who are part of Keswick today, and then to look at the results of the revival, in terms of its impact in the principality of Wales and beyond Wales – in fact a worldwide influence. Then I want to draw some conclusions.

Being open to the Spirit

There are many ways in which the Spirit touches people's lives but there is a responsibility on us, as God's people, to be open to the Spirit coming in power. This has often been the message, at Keswick, throughout the years. In 1903, before the revival in Wales took off, F. B. Meyer, a major Keswick speaker, was talking at the Convention about Jesus as the One who overwhelms us with the Holy Ghost, who baptises us with the Holy Ghost. This kind of language was being used before the revival came.

What is revival? Here is a possible definition

A revival is a sovereign outpouring of the Holy Spirit upon a group of Christians resulting in their spiritual revival and quickening, and

---

[2] Kevin Adams, *A Diary of Revival: the outbreak of the 1904 Welsh Awakening*, (Farnham: CWR, 2004). The book is available in two forms and there is a video and a DVD.

issuing in the awakening of spiritual concern in outsiders or formal church members; an immediate, or, at other times a more long term effect will be efforts to extend the influence of the Kingdom of God both intensively in the society in which the Church is placed, and extensively in the spread of the gospel to more remote parts of the world.[3]

I think that is a good definition. We could argue about some of the finer points, but that describes what happened in Wales. Revival is more than simply the renewal of the church. The renewal of the church is important, but revival goes on to affect society. The revival of 1904–5 affected Welsh society; which at that time was, in any case, in a process of change, by injecting new things into the life of Wales. The principality, and beyond, was deeply affected by the revival. There was a background of theological liberalism in many of the churches in Wales before the revival. Preaching was often academic, it might be from the Bible but it did not stir the hearts of people. There was a decline in church membership and many people were concerned about the moral and spiritual state of the country.

One danger, in thinking about revival, is that we can focus, purely, on waiting for God to do something – the sovereign aspect, God's direct action. That is crucial, but it is also important not to neglect the human agents. On the other hand, historians who are not Christians tend to give all the weight, when they speak about revival phenomena, to explanations about cultural change and the way in which people are in a state of dislocation and are, therefore, open to religious influences. Certainly the background must not be neglected. Social and political developments are important, but I would argue that because this revival actually spread far beyond Wales, to many other countries, we cannot explain it simply in terms of what was going on in Welsh society. Otherwise it would have been totally contained within that society.

Keswick itself was actually a product of a time of awakening in the nineteenth century. But Keswick's immediate focus, when it began,

---

[3]   R. E. Davies, *I will pour out my Spirit: a history and theology of revivals and evangelical awakenings* (Tunbridge Wells: Monarch, 1992).

was not the evangelisation of the lost or wider awakening. It was the inner reviving of believers. At a time when many evangelical believers were feeling the struggles of spiritual life, Keswick came on the scene, with its message of a deeper consecration to God. Revival meetings proliferated through the nineteenth century. Organisations like the Evangelical Alliance, in the nineteenth century, were holding weeks of prayer. All of this was preparing the way for Keswick and was going to link to the Welsh revival.

What leads to revival?

I want to move to some of the things that led to revival. I see this as important because in our desire for God to work in greater power in this country our responsibility is to pray and also seek to prepare the way. Keswick played a part in the Welsh revival and who knows what part Keswick could play again – and perhaps is already playing?

A heightened expectation of God at work

In 1903 a Keswick-style Convention was held in Wales, for the first time – in Llandrindod Wells – and this was one of the streams which led to the Welsh revival. People from Wales were already attending the Keswick Convention and they wanted to have the message spread to Wales. Some Welsh ministers, in particular, spoke about this. Rhys Davies, one of them, talked to a group of ministers and theological students. And they became convinced that a 'Keswick in Wales' was in God's will. Davies announced, in 1902, that the Convention would be going to Wales and that church leaders would be influenced.[4]

Prayer circles

A second influence was prayer and preaching circles in Wales, which included powerful preachers, such as Seth Joshua, who were calling

---

[4] For links between Keswick and Revival, see C. M. Price and I. M. Randall, *Transforming Keswick* (Carlisle: Paternoster/OM, 2000).

Christians to more consecrated living and meaningful prayer. Seth became an itinerant evangelist, going around Wales holding missions. He stressed not only people coming to Christ but deeper consecration to Christ, a crucifixion of self. He spoke about the power of Pentecost, joy in God, and active service for Christ. So this was a second strand leading to the revival.

The female touch

Thirdly, the influence of women was significant in the lead-up to the revival and in the revival itself. An effective evangelist, in the period before 1904 was Rosina Davies. She had been affected by the Salvation Army and its teaching on holiness and she would often see 20 people, and sometimes as many as 50 people converted in a single meeting. This was before what we would call the Welsh revival proper had started. Things were bubbling up.

Another lady who was involved was Jessie Penn-Lewis, who was an important Keswick figure. Her father had been a minister in Glamorganshire and she settled, with her husband, in Richmond in Surrey. Jessie Penn-Lewis had a profound experience of the Holy Spirit and she brought this to messages that she gave at Keswick. She spoke to women's meetings but she was not content with just speaking to the women. She was a driving force behind the Welsh Keswick Convention, in Llandrindod Wells, and was a strategic thinker. She recommended as speakers at Llandrindod Wells a Methodist, a Baptist and an Anglican. In her mind, this was not about one denomination, but was about God's Spirit, moving across the denominations. There was an impulse connected with a greater scope for women to exercise their ministry.

Ministers seek revival

Another factor was young ministers seeking personal revival, seeking to be filled with the Holy Spirit. One of them, Owen Owen, wrote on behalf of a group of young ministers to F. B. Meyer, who was a very well-known minister in London, saying, 'Can you help us?' Meyer told the group to go to the 1903 Llandrindod Wells Convention. Meyer gave an opportunity, at the final meeting of this convention, for expressions of fresh dedication to God. *The Life of Faith*, which reported all these conventions, said that it seemed as if everyone in the tent wanted to receive 'the fullness of God's blessing.'[5] That was another channel.

F.B. Meyer was a little cautious about Welsh emotionalism and he wanted to insist that this 'infilling' was not just an emotional experience. Submission to the authority of God was necessary. One of the young Baptist ministers who was there, R.B. Jones, went on to have a long ministry in Wales, which really refutes the idea that the Welsh revival was a short-lived wonder. R.B. Jones spoke to F.B. Meyer about his great need to be filled with the Holy Spirit, to be caught up in what he said was a flood that he felt they were going to experience in Wales. He was waiting for more and more, he said, 'and there is more and more of God.' These ministers felt themselves to be totally changed by what they had experienced and they became leaders in revival missions.

The revival takes off – autumn 1904

These various streams came together in September 1904. Seth Joshua went to a significant conference, in Blaenannerch, Cardiganshire, one of a series of small meetings for the deepening of spiritual life. He was a discerning preacher and felt that a new spiritual current was beginning to be felt in Wales in the autumn of 1904. Two other people at the meetings were also going to be significant. One of them was Joseph Jenkins, a minister in Newquay. He had been affected by the Llandrindod Wells convention of 1903 and began to preach in a more powerful way in his own church. He spent hours praying, especially for the young people of his church and encouraged them to take part in the services, to give testimony to the things that God was doing in their lives.

One of the young people, Florrie Evans, aged twenty, was seeking to acknowledge before the people the Lordship of Christ over her life

---

[5]   *The Life of Faith*, 12 August 1903, p. 572.

and to submit to the Holy Spirit. At one of the young people's meetings, when about sixty young people were present, Florrie said, simply, 'I love the Lord Jesus with all my heart.' The result was electrifying. Seth Joshua noted the Spirit that had come upon these people because of that testimony. There is a lesson here not to despise the small things, the ways in which God is at work in some young person's life. Groups of young people, some working within the Christian Endeavour movement, were to constitute a key element in the revival. This was to be both a strength and, at times, a weakness, but these young people were at the forefront of a number of the significant things that happened.

Amongst these young people, the leader was Evan Roberts, who was at the conference in Cardiganshire and was to become the best known figure of the revival. As the revival proceeded, the press reports concentrated attention on Evan Roberts, a twenty-six-year-old. Roberts had been a miner for 12 years and then an apprentice blacksmith. From his teens, he had been a devoted member of his local chapel, Moriah, in Loughor. He had been seeking God for years as a younger person. And Seth Joshua had prayed that God would take and use 'A lad from the coal mine or from the fields.' – not somebody who came through the established routes of theological training. Evan had in fact already started his theological training, but he was to be the answer to that prayer. He had not only studied the Bible deeply for himself but also had studied outlines of theology. Within these years of preparation, there had grown within him a desire to preach the gospel and to see people won to Christ. These conferences for deeper spiritual life in 1903 attracted Roberts. People could share with one another and could hear God speaking to them.

On the 29th September 1904, at one of the evening meetings at Blaenannerch, Roberts was deeply affected by a prayer by Seth Joshua, in which he included the words, 'Lord, bend us.' Roberts was led to pray, in deep anguish of Spirit, 'Bend me.' A new and overwhelming experience of God's Spirit came on him. He lost the nervousness that he had had in speaking and he began to mobilise others. There were plans for some young people to constitute a mission team and they were to play a prominent part in the revival.

Revival meetings

Evan Roberts had a vision of Jesus Christ presenting a sort of cheque to God the Father, on which was written: 100,000. Evan Roberts and others began to pray for 100,000 conversions to take place in Wales. All the reliable estimates suggest that this figure was surpassed. Evan Roberts and his team began to take meetings in the chapels of various denominations across the valleys of South Wales, speaking to people about the need to repent, to confess sin, to look to Christ, to put away sin, to obey the Spirit, to become witnesses to Christ. There was a stress on assurance of faith and on sheer joy in God. In one year, 1905, the membership of Baptist churches in England and Wales increased by 30,000. In addition, in many places the inner life of congregations was renewed.

On 28th of October 1904, Roberts wrote in his diary 'Before I came to Newcastle Emlyn, I never met young ladies who could and were willing to speak of religious things. The old fashion was to draw a long face when speaking of religious things. But it was most part of it hypocrisy, and based on the fact and thought that God is a solemn and just God, and at the same time forgetting that God is a happy God and a joyful God.'[6] This is typical of the bluntness of Evan Roberts, a bluntness which could sometimes get him into deep trouble.

Evan Roberts become the most sought-after itinerant preacher around Cardiganshire and beyond. Meetings filling the chapels, sometimes a thousand or more people crowding into chapels. Meetings going on for hours and hours, often into the early hours of the morning. Many people, including many miners, were dramatically converted, and we have the testimonies of these people. They were overwhelmed with the power of the Holy Spirit. People

---

[6]   K. Adams, *A Diary of Revival*, p. 79.

testified, there and then. There was, admittedly, much emotion. Roberts would go among the congregation, praying with people, and other team members joined him. The meetings were not carefully organised. Many things happened, some of them not so helpful, but many of them very good.

Roberts did preach, but he did not always preach traditional sermons. He spoke very directly to the people, sometimes even to individuals within the congregations. He allowed interruptions and then he would use the interruptions to make his message even plainer than it had been before. There was a great deal of singing at the meetings, led particularly by the young women in Roberts' team such as Annie Davies, aged eighteen. Occasionally, when the singers thought a sermon was going on a very long time, they would start up some singing to vary the pace. There were visions of what God was going to do, direct guidance (perhaps not all of it well founded), healing and prophecies.

During the meetings Roberts would often pray, 'Send the Spirit, more powerfully, for Jesus' sake.'[7] There was a great sense of freedom, particularly in the early months of the revival. But with these daily long meetings and lack of sleep, Evan Roberts, particularly, became utterly exhausted. He didn't look after himself well and, as he lost his physical energy, he seemed to lose some of the energy of the Spirit. He could be very judgemental about those who did not appear to be submitting to the Spirit. After a couple of years he withdrew to a large extent from his public ministry – but these were amazing years.

Keswick and the revival

As Keswick was a part of the nurturing of the early seeds of the revival, so the revival itself came back to Keswick. A contingent of about three hundred people from Wales came to the Keswick Convention in 1905, fresh from their experiences. Special meetings

---

7   K. Adams, *A Diary of Revival*, p. 99.

were arranged at the Convention in that year in which the Welsh were able to, as it said in one of the reports, have 'free play for their enthusiasm'. There were many testimonies, there was extra singing, and prayer went on, at some of those Convention meetings, until three o'clock in the morning. Later in that particular week of the Convention, there was an evening session with A.T. Pierson, from America, as the speaker. Before he started speaking, he called on all those who had felt God's refining fire to stand up, and everyone in the tent stood up. Pierson never began his message; instead prayer went on for two and a half hours, with calls for God's power. But, naturally enough, there were people who had mixed feelings about what was going on.

In Wales itself, one minister, Peter Price, wrote very critically about the revival, even describing some of the meetings as 'a sham.' He argued that there was a real revival but that it was possible to be so diverted into some of the external exhibitions that it would become a bogus revival, and he called for discernment. It was right that he should do so. Discernment was essential. Another Keswick figure who spoke about the difficulties was J.B. Figgis: 'The torrent,' he said, 'from the Welsh hills meeting the sluggish stream of English propriety threatened tumult.'[8] So there we have it; the clash of spiritual cultures. Sometimes people on the Convention platform were having to deal with this; on the one hand, a wave of emotion, and on the other hand, a need to keep the exposition of Scripture central. The direct Welsh influence on the main Keswick Convention was relatively short lived and later people were talking, in very approving terms, of a quiet and solemn Convention, that had taken place a couple of years later.

The problems of revival

There were divisions over certain revival phenomena. This is often a feature of revival. Some people think, 'If only revival would come, all

---

[8]   J.B. Figgis, *Keswick from Within* (London, 1914), p. 151.

our problems would be over.' Not so. Divisions opened up, and in some cases situations became quite tense. Some people, especially R.B. Jones, became respected preachers, and were much honoured, but others went for the externals of revival. There was a vogue, for a period, of having meetings at which there was no chairman; they called it 'meetings with the empty chair' – which was simply to say 'the Holy Spirit is in charge'. This was hardly the way to ensure the Holy Spirit's blessing – just by having an empty chair and no chairman.

Evan Roberts, by 1908, was beginning to come back into some of these meetings. A *Life and Faith* report spoke about a meeting which he addressed. There was a desire to keep some revival elements going, and at the same time a recognition that meetings could not go on in exactly the same way. Most people in Wales did not agree with the criticisms that were made of the revival. Many people saw its positive benefits, and in much of the Welsh press the revival received enthusiastic coverage. I think that is very significant. Those writing in the press spoke about the great crowds of people and saw the benefits that ensued.

Eifion Evans makes an interesting point: he believes that the Welsh revival was not allowed to be Welsh enough. Some people, he argues, tried to take it over and turn it into something else. True Christian spirituality has to work within the context in which we are. We cannot just translate a spirituality into another context and think it will automatically work. Many people have tried to do that.

How did this affect Welsh society?

A true revival affects the wider society. Kevin Adams speaks about the stories of the miners who responded in droves to the message; about dramatic changes taking place in the way that people lived and worked. The pit ponies could not understand the new language that the miners were speaking; the swear-free phrases totally confused them. The work ethic was transformed; the colliers put in a better day's work. And although some of the owners had been frightened that enthusiastic prayer meetings would take up all the working time, there was reconciliation between management and workers. People who had been rather poor in paying bills, settled them. Feuds in local communities were settled. Effects were felt in homes. Children prayed for their parents – because many of these first converts were young people. For many mothers, who had seen the money of the home go on beer, this money was transformed into housekeeping money. Chronic alcohol problems were solved. Magistrates sometimes had no cases to hear in the courts. One inspector of the NSPCC said that homes under his observation, where there had been cruelty to children, had undergone a complete transformation through the parents having been brought to a better life.

Preachers of the time spoke about these social changes, but it is also the case that many of the preachers encouraged people not to get involved in society and instead to channel all their energies into spiritual things, in a narrower sense. I consider that this was a downside of the revival, as it went on. And many Welsh Nonconformists swung to the idea of a rather social gospel, almost as a reaction against this other-worldliness of the revival. Not all of what happened helped to sustain long-term spiritual change in Welsh society.

The spread beyond Wales

Many people visited Wales and spoke about the power that they saw in the meetings. F.B. Meyer went down from London to hear Evan Roberts. At one meeting, when Roberts was praying with considerable fervour, a man sitting next to F.B. Meyer said, 'We don't want to listen to all this, let's start a hymn to drown it out.' Meyer blurted out, 'Drown it man? I've come all the way from London to catch it.' He wanted to absorb something of what was going on and take it back to London.

Large revival meetings were held in London and in other parts of England. The General Secretary of the Baptist Union organised meetings in London. Campbell Morgan, of Westminster Chapel, was part of this venture. Dinsdale Young, of the Westminster Central Hall, and Thomas Spurgeon, of the Metropolitan Tabernacle, were among the ministers holding meetings and saying, 'We want to see this happening in London.' The rector of All Souls, Langham Place, attended. Gipsy Smith, the Methodist, was involved. One Baptist minister said, 'I seemed to be searched through and through, by the white light of the Spirit of holiness.' Many local churches and many regions of England were affected. The Berkshire Baptist Association reported 200 baptisms in the churches. A mission was convened at the Metropolitan Tabernacle, in London, with students from Spurgeon's college – Welsh students had come back from Wales and brought back news of what was happenings in their villages. The Principal of Spurgeon's College said, 'We must harness this movement, we must have a mission in the Elephant and Castle area.' Hundreds of people were converted through this mission.

You can read in the helpful book by Noel Gibbard, *On the Wings of a Dove*[9], about revival movements that developed in France, Russia, Scandinavia, Armenia, Turkey and elsewhere. Welsh missionaries went out across the world; some people think thousands of missionaries, over a number of years. Meetings in Algeria, in this period, conducted by a French pastor who had been touched by the revival, attracted many thousands. There was, therefore, a wave of the Holy Spirit across many countries. Amy Carmichael, a Keswick missionary in south-west India, spoke of people in her Dohnavur community, hearing about the revival, wanting to see the Spirit of God move, and lying on the floor crying out to God. Conversions were taking place, and Christians were quickened.

Pandita Ramabai, another outstanding Christian in India, from a distinguished Hindu family, had established a centre for young widows and orphans, called Mukti, meaning salvation. She heard about what had happened at the Welsh revival. She wanted to see, as she said at Keswick, 'A thousand Spirit-filled Indian women to

---

[9]   Noel Gibbard, *On the Wings of a Dove: the international effects of the 1904–05 Revival* (Bridgend: Bryntirion Press, 2002).

empower other Indian women, to go through India', and to see reformation and revival in her own country. When she heard about the Welsh revival, she started prayer circles. Girls and women, in this Mukti community, were praying for revival and an empowering of the Spirit came to them. There was weeping, confession of sins, and prayers for others. A visiting Brethren evangelist, G.H. Lang, said he was part of the community for a period and spoke of people lost for hours in praise and expressions of love for Jesus. This was not a short-term revival; the effects were felt for a considerable time in India and elsewhere.

Pentecostalism

It is well known that the Pentecostal movement emerged in Los Angeles in 1906 but it is sometimes overlooked that it had strong links with the Welsh revival. F.B. Meyer spoke for eight days to large audiences in Los Angeles in 1906 about the Welsh revival. One of those present spoke about a group of people being stirred as they heard what was going on in Wales. Donald Gee, the leading Pentecostal historian, says that the Welsh revival helped people to visualise a return to apostolic Christianity. This was what Pentecostalism took up.

A number of people in Los Angeles embraced the thought that God was doing a new thing, and started prayer meetings to pray for the outpouring of the Spirit. These prayer meetings ran for a number of weeks. A black holiness preacher, William Seymour, was called to pastor one of the new congregations that emerged, the Azusa Street Mission. This mixed congregation became the well-spring of world-wide Pentecostalism. There what had been experienced in the Welsh revival was experienced again. The Pentecostal movement, through people like the Jeffreys brothers, who were converted in the Welsh revival, spread with great rapidity.

What can we learn from the Welsh revival?

The first thing is to note that there are always factors that contribute to a revival. There are many different contributory elements, some to do with the society around, but, above all, there are people who are seeking God. This is a marked feature of all revivals; the desire of people for spiritual change, for change in their churches, for change in their societies. We may say, 'How would this happen today?' There are some remarkable things happening in our own country and across Europe. I have seen some of the ways God is working in parts of Eastern Europe. Some of you have seen it elsewhere, in the two-thirds world. It is very significant what is happening in the black majority churches in this country today. The growth, the dynamic, the power of the Spirit, the number of conversions – that is one place that we can look to see the seeds of God at work in significant ways. Also in the gipsy communities in this country and in other countries, the percentage of Christians is considerable higher than it is in the wider community. People in different contexts are hungering for God.

In the second place, often as revival takes off, young people, largely inexperienced, find themselves in leadership. There is a vulnerability about this process and yet I suggest we need to be open to this happening. Sometimes mistakes will be made, phenomena will not be handled well, preaching will not be exactly as we would like it, and yet that energy of the Spirit in young people and in inexperienced people has to be channelled in a positive way. There has to be openness, I believe, to the possibility of God doing things in new ways, in different ways. The Welsh revival in some ways was disorganised, even chaotic. Sometimes God breaks open the mould of the ways in which we have traditionally worked.

Finally, connections are important, since revival spreads as people speak to other people, as people are prayed for by others. Each of us, to use the title of one of the biographies of Evan Roberts, can be an instrument of God's Spirit, an 'instrument of revival'. But because people are involved there are always some problems. Revival is not the answer to all the difficulties of the church. Indeed it can cause divisions between churches. Ultimately, however, revival is not designed so that we in the churches can feel good. It is about the needy world knowing salvation in Christ. This is what Evan Roberts said, on 10th October 1904. He wrote, 'The wheels of the gospel chariot are to turn rapidly ere long. And to be permitted to have a hand with the cause is a privilege.' For this power of the gospel we rightly pray.

Keswick Lecture – Week 2

Finding Certainty in an Uncertain World

by *Michael Ramsden*

MICHAEL RAMSDEN

Born in England and raised in the Middle East, Michael became a Christian while living in Cyprus. From the moment of his conversion he wanted to be an evangelist. At the age of twenty-six he set up a European office for Ravi Zacharias International Ministries. Since then he has travelled widely in Europe, the Middle East, India, the Far East, North America and South Africa, speaking at universities, churches and conferences. Michael enjoys photography, reading and fast cars. He is married to Anne and they have three young children, Lucy, James and Amelia.

Finding Certainty in an Uncertain World

Introduction

The topic which I have selected to speak on is a vast one, and there is a large amount which I won't be able to discuss in detail. To begin with, I want to outline the many different kinds of uncertainty in our world. Then I'd like to concentrate on one in particular which I think is the major cause why both Christians and non-Christians feel troubled in their hearts and wonder if anything can be certain, in any way whatsoever.

Philosophical uncertainty

There is a general philosophical uncertainty that has its roots in scepticism, which tells you that you can never be certain of anything. A few years ago, I was speaking to a group of very high powered MOD officials, in an after dinner talk. At the end of it, it was thrown open to questions and the very first comment that was made, from the most senior person, was 'You can never be certain of anything, can you?' I looked at him and said, 'Are you certain about that?' He said, 'What I was trying to say was there's no such thing as truth.' And I said, 'Do you believe that to be true?' At this point, he said, 'I seem to be in difficulty.' I said, 'I think you are.'

The conviction that there is no such thing as truth has led many to conclude therefore that there is no point in asking questions. The point of asking a question is in order to find an answer and if there are no answers, what *is* the point of asking questions? We now live in a culture which is marked by the fact, not that it has simply lost the answers to life's big questions, but it has stopped asking the questions themselves and therefore doesn't even know what the questions are any more.

This move is fundamentally flawed for the very simple reason that if you say, 'There is no such thing as truth', you are arguing that it is true there is no such thing as truth. But if it is true there is no such thing as truth, then it is not true there is no such thing as truth, because what you have just said is true. But if it is not true that there is no such thing as truth, then it is not true there is no such thing as truth, so what you have said is not true. You have said nothing but in a complicated way.

This is why one philosopher, by the name of Scruton, said, 'When someone tells you, "There is no such thing as truth," they are asking you not to believe them. So don't.'

Historical uncertainty

Laying aside this general philosophical uncertainty, we also have what we could call a historical uncertainty. Many years ago now, I found myself sitting opposite a professor of history and I said to him, 'What kind of history do you teach?' He said, 'I teach postmodern history.' I said, 'What is postmodern history?' He said, 'All history is a question of interpretation, facts don't interpret themselves. All history tells you is what the historian thinks about what happened. History books don't tell you what happened, they tell you what someone wants you to believe happened.' I said, 'Is this an examined course at your university?' And his face fell. He said, 'It used to be but students wrote whatever they wanted to in the exam.'

Ontological uncertainty

To compound it even further, we have what we could call an ontological uncertainty. Ontology is to do with what exists and what doesn't. I used to teach moral philosophy and epistemology at a university. Every single year, without fail, in every tutorial, at the beginning of every new group, someone would ask the question, 'How do I know I exist?' I gave a stock answer I heard from someone else. I'd look at them, lower my glasses and say, 'Who shall I say is asking?'

Linguistic uncertainty

We now have a linguistic uncertainty that is dominant in our culture where we actually believe that language itself has lost meaning and that reason and meaning are simply a complex construct of grammar; which is arbitrary, with no fixed points of reference and therefore cannot ultimately convey anything in a concrete way.

Theological uncertainty

Not only do we have philosophical uncertainty, historical uncertainty, ontological uncertainty and linguistic uncertainty – sadly now, in some evangelical circles, we have introduced a level of theological uncertainty, along the lines of 'Does God know the future?' Even, to put it more accurately, 'Is there a future which God can actually know?' As if, somehow, God would find it difficult actually to know what happens before it occurs. This has become an incredibly complex area. But you will find four places, in the Greek New Testament, where we are told that God existed before time itself began. The two most strong would be in 2 Timothy 1:9 and Titus 1:2. 2 Timothy says, 'προ χρονων αιωνιων – *Pro chronon aionion.*' Titus says '*Pro chronon aionion.*' Did you hear the difference? There isn't any. It says, *Theo* – God; who exists, *pro* – before; *chronon* – time, *aionion* – age: before the age of time itself, God did this. We worship a God who exists outside of time itself and if God exists outside of time itself and he is the Author of space and time, what difficulty would he have in knowing the future, since all of space, time, history is stretched out before him?

Some people feel that there's a degree of tyranny in this, that God knows everything that will happen before it happens, he is in charge of everything. But let me say there has never been a time, in Christian theology, when somebody has been able to commit adultery, climb out of the adultery bed, get on their knees and say, 'Lord, why did you predestine me to commit adultery, before time began? I hope that you are ashamed of what you made me do and when I get to heaven, I will await your apology.' That has never been part of Christian theology. We're morally responsible but there is a future which is fixed and it gives us hope, not despair.

Moral uncertainty

However, none of these, I think, are the greatest single cause of the rampant uncertainty that we find in our world today. The greatest degree of uncertainty that troubles the human heart in the west today is moral uncertainty. I do not mean uncertainty as to what morals are, although there is a lot of debate about that. By moral uncertainty, I mean that we are not certain whether it is a morally good thing, as Christians, to believe what we do and to be certain that we do. Isn't there something immoral in that stance? And the world is troubled by anyone who believes they have the truth, especially when it comes to forms of absolute morality. That makes them feel nervous and the only solution to it is to introduce a degree of uncertainty.

I spend a lot of my time working as an evangelist and as an apologist. That doesn't mean that I evangelise people and then apologise to them. I spend most of my time in front of non-Christian audiences, being pelted with their questions. People find this strangely attractive and think they're going to be able to ask a question to sink Christianity. It never occurs to anybody that, for 2,000 years, someone's being trying to think of a question to sink Christianity and, for 2,000 years, they've failed. They come and ask many questions and I do my best to answer them.

At the end of one event, a few months ago, a lady came up to me and said, 'I was troubled by what you had to say. You seemed to imply, in everything you were saying, that there is only one way to heaven. I can't accept that. I am a Buddhist.' And I said, 'You're telling me you don't want to consider the claims of Christ because

Christianity is exclusive, so you're a Buddhist instead?' She said, 'Yes.' I said, 'Didn't Buddha reject the Vedas, as the divine revelation of God, from the Hindu system and also reject the caste system? If Buddha was here today, he would tell you that over one billion Hindus are wrong in their fundamental beliefs.' Her mouth fell open. She said, 'That's true, I read it last week.' I said, 'If you're prepared to entertain Buddha, who was exclusive in his claims to truth, then why not also be prepared to entertain Christ?' She said, 'I don't like where this conversation is going. I don't want to become an intolerant person.' Do you hear what she's saying? 'I want to be a morally good person. Becoming a Christian will not make me morally better; it will make me morally worse.'

Monism

I don't know if many of you are familiar with a thinker by the name of Isaiah Berlin. Isaiah Berlin was one of the great intellectual figures who dominated life at Oxford University in the last century and is still a dominant force in many schools of thought around the world today. Isaiah Berlin had two main areas of study. They were to do with freedom and what he called 'monism'. Freedom: the idea that somehow we should be free, to engage in the ends that we want to. And monism: the idea that there is just one, universal truth, into which all other truths must be made to fit.

The reason he had these two is that they were deeply and intimately connected, because 'the enemy of freedom,' Isaiah Berlin argued, 'is monism. The ancient belief that there is a single harmony of truths, into which everything else, if it is genuine, must be made to fit; the consequences of this belief are the root of all evil. Because it means that those who know should command those who do not. To cause pain, to kill, to torture are, in a general, rightly condemned; but if these things are done, not for my personal benefit but for some ism – socialism, nationalism, fascism, communism, some fanatically held religious belief, then they are permissible under the monist system.' Which is why, he goes on to say, 'monism is one step away from despotism.' 'If you have someone,' says Isaiah Berlin, 'who believes they know the truth and who believes they know the way in which other people should live, such a person is a despot.' Isn't that what the communists tried to do? Isn't that what the fascists tried to do? And didn't they all do incredibly terrible things, in the name of their ism? 'And how are evangelical Christians different from that?' Isaiah Berlin would say. 'Don't you believe you have the truth? Don't you believe you know how other people should live? Are you, therefore, not one step away from despotism?'

I can remember when I was reading him articulating this, so eloquently because he wrote so beautifully, at the end I wrote a simple sentence, which said, 'What about a monism filled with grace?'

This idea is one that has taken a deep root in so many people's hearts, in the west. It troubles them that people believe they can be certain because, in the name of certainty, atrocities are committed. Surely, the response to that is to be uncertain, less certain?

Almost every question that I get asked, against the Christian faith, is, at root, a moral question. It is a moral complaint, against God – 'Isn't it morally wrong of God to do something?' The simple truth is that every time someone raises a complaint against God, they are raising a moral complaint against God and it is monist in its nature. They are claiming to give you a moral truth with which God himself must also comply and, if he doesn't, he is evil. Many people reject God today because they look at the world, they see everything happening around them, they are troubled in their hearts and they think, 'I cannot be certain.'

Many Christians feel that they will become intolerant people if they boldly proclaim the truth. Since when is intolerance listed as one of the fruits of the Spirit or been part of the fruit of the Spirit? Did it appear on your list? When's the last time you sang a chorus that worshipped God for being a despot? Moral confusion as to the nature of making an exclusive claim, or as to the character of God, will always lead in gross uncertainty. I'm wondering if you are embarrassed as a Christian, because you think there is some fundamental moral problem with the kind of certainty that Christ offered.

A threat or a promise?

I want to change track slightly and then try and pull it all together at the end. Let me read to you from Isaiah chapter 1.

> The vision concerning Judah and Jerusalem that Isaiah son of Amoz saw during the reigns of Uzziah, Jotham, Ahaz and Hezekiah, kings of Judah.

> Hear, O heavens! Listen, O earth!
> For the LORD has spoken:
> 'I reared children and brought them up,
> but they have rebelled against me.
> The ox knows his master,
> the donkey his owner's manger,
> but Israel does not know,
> my people do not understand.'

> Ah, sinful nation,
> a people loaded with guilt,
> a brood of evildoers,
> children given to corruption!
> They have forsaken the LORD;
> they have spurned the Holy One of Israel
> and turned their backs on him.

> Why should you be beaten any more?
> Why do you persist in rebellion?
> Your whole head is injured,
> your whole heart afflicted.
> From the sole of your foot to the top of your head.
> There is no soundness–
> only wounds and welts
> and open sores,
> not cleansed or bandaged
> or soothed with oil.

What did you hear? Did you hear a threat and the promise of judgement? Or did you hear something else?

I get asked this question so often: 'The God of the Old Testament is this vengeful, wrath-filled God and the God of the New Testament is this God of love. It's almost like God tries being angry for a few thousand years and that didn't work. So he changed jobs, had some PR consultancy and thought "Why don't we project a new image?" And then out comes this loving God of the New Testament.' Is that true?

Let me read to you Jonah's complaint against God. Jonah's angry with God too.

> But Jonah was greatly displeased and became angry. He prayed to the LORD, 'O LORD, is this not what I said when I was still at home? That is why I was so quick to flee to Tarshish. I knew that you are a gracious and compassionate God, slow to anger and abounding in love, a God who relents from sending calamity. Now, O LORD, take away my life, for it is better for me to die than to live.'

What is Jonah's complaint against God's moral character? That he is a loving, gracious and compassionate God. That's his whole problem. This dichotomy between the Old and New Testaments is so false, it's almost embarrassing to mention it. But because it's so dominant in so many minds, it means every single time we read the Old Testament, that's what we're expecting to hear, so everything is then filtered through those windows.

What did you just hear? Was it a threat or was it a promise? We live in a world that wants to be free. Free from what? The answer you'll most commonly get is, 'Free from external constraint, especially free from the shackles of morality.' But freedom is not doing whatever you want, whenever you want, however you want to. That is not freedom, that is anarchy. Freedom is a moral concept: it only exists within a moral framework. Take freedom outside of the moral framework, within which it was given, and you do not end up with more freedom, you end up with anarchy.

The cost of moral failure

Quite often, I get asked to speak to high-powered businessmen and women and one question that they will always have in the back of their minds is, 'Can I afford to be moral, as a business person? Surely, by not being moral, I am more free to make more money. Therefore there is a cost of compliance with morality.' And it is true – there is an economic cost of compliance with morality. But there's a higher cost to be factored in.

After the terrorist attacks of September 11th in 2001, stock markets around the world fell dramatically. Many people don't realise that by January 2002, they had largely recovered to their former position. In February 2002, the Worldcom and Enron scandals broke. Stock markets fell further and faster, around the world, than they did in the light of the terrorist attacks of September 11th, telling you that investors believe that the greatest single threat to western economic stability is not a terrorist attack from without but a moral collapse from within. There is a cost of compliance, economically, with morality but the cost of failure is catastrophic.

I was asked to go and speak to a very high-powered group of people, at one of the largest banks in the world. There was just 15 people in the room. Between them, they had tens of billions of dollars; half of them owned it and the other half were investing it. They asked me to speak to them about Enron, which I did because it was my specialist research area. When I got to the end of my talk, one of them said, 'Michael, when do you believe stock markets will recover?' This is a grossly unfair question. The people in that room get paid more every day than I earn every year to answer these questions. So, after pointing this out to them, I said, 'That's very simple. If you believe the kinds of moral failures you've seen, with Enron and Worldcom, are one-offs, you can expect a stock market recovery any time soon. But if you believe this kind of moral collapse and failure, within corporations, is endemic, it's going to take at least ten of fifteen years for them to recover.'

All of the colour drained out of everybody's face and I left that room thinking, 'Now's a good time to sell.'

In the Old Testament, God tells us that he detests inaccurate weights and measures. Israel was an agricultural community. Accurate weights and measures were the fundamental unit of account, by which the value of anything could be measured and determined. If a moral failure occurred, in this basic unit of account, the whole system would collapse, which is why God spoke so frequently against it. Was it a threat or a promise? It was a promise. If you live this way, this is what you will reap. What did we just read in Isaiah, was it a threat or a promise? Did you hear the pathos of God's heart, in this speech? 'Why should you be beaten any more?'

As someone once said, 'It is impossible to break God's moral law.' It is impossible to break God's moral law, in this sense. Supposing you wanted to break the law of gravity. You climbed to the top of this tent, you tie a red cape around your shoulder and you put on a pair of red underpants, on the outside of the rest of your clothing, and you throw yourself from the top, in an attempt to break the law of gravity. Will you break the law of gravity? What will you break? It is impossible to break God's moral law, you simply break yourself, while proving his law in the very process.

What is freedom?

God created a world, in which he wanted freedom. That's why, in the gospel, it says, 'It was for freedom that [you were set] free.' But freedom is a moral concept, it only exists within a moral framework. God gave us a moral system, not because he wanted to imprison us but because he wanted to free us. Every time you live in contradiction to God's moral law, you do not so much break his law, as you break yourself in the process.

Have you ever been betrayed? Lied to? Cheated? Stabbed in the back by a friend? Did it hurt? Every time God's moral law is broken, we are broken. We live in a broken world, surrounded by broken people, with broken lives. But did you hear what God is saying in Isaiah? 'Why do you want to be beaten any more? Why do you want to live like this? Why? Why do you persist in your rebellion? Why?'

The most common reason Christians and non-Christians break God's moral law is they want to be happy – but breaking God's moral law will not make you happy. It will make you broken.

That's why Jesus wept over Jerusalem. Breaking God's moral law didn't just break us and break this world and break everything else around us – it also broke God's heart. Which is why later in Isaiah, God says, 'Come now, let us reason together ... Though your sins are like scarlet, they shall be as white as snow.' Do you hear God's heart in this? This is not a threat, this is a promise. It's like saying to somebody, 'You are walking towards the edge of a cliff, another five steps, you're going to fall off. You will tumble down the mountain-side, doing untold damage and then you will be splattered on the rocks below.' Is that a threat or a promise? It's a promise.

When we see untold horrors in this world, it should not cause us to doubt God – we should doubt God if we do not see these things happening in the world and in our lives and in the lives of people around us. Because if they were not happening, we should doubt God because then God would be a liar – and what he tells us will happen to us, if we persist in our rebellion, would not be true. Suffering in no way should make us question God's character but it should make us question ours.

Parents sometimes ask very stupid questions. 'Do you want a smack?' It's a rhetorical question, isn't it? These are rhetorical questions. 'Why should you be beaten? Why?' Can you give me a single good reason why you should suffer what is described here in Isaiah? So why persist living in that way?

The nature of faith

A lot of us misunderstand the nature of faith. Faith, to believe something by faith, is not a philosophical speculation, grounded in fantasy. Has anyone ever said to you, 'I'm so happy you believe what you believe. I wish I could believe what you believe but I can't.' Have you ever stopped to ask yourself what they exactly mean by that? We heard it said yesterday, by Jonathan Lamb: 'Faith is believing in what you know isn't true.' What do you call people who believe in things that are not there? Mad people. So, when someone says this to you, they are saying, 'Look, you are actually insane for believing this but the main thing is that you are happy and insane and I am happy that you are happy. I am so desperate to be happy myself, I too would embrace insanity, if I thought it would get me there but I just can't do it.'

The Bible says that faith is a gift. It is not the gift of stupidity. In Greek there are two words which you can use for faith, *pistis* and *nomizo*. When you read your Bible, every single time you see the word 'faith' translated, it doesn't matter what translation you have, it will always be the Greek word *pistis* behind it. Because *nomizo* is never ever translated 'faith' in the New Testament, it's used very sparingly and almost entirely in a negative context. Now this is very important. For the Hellenistic and classical Greeks, whenever they described faith in their own gods, they used the word *nomizo*. It comes from the Greek word *nomos*, which means law, custom, habit, it is a belief they have inherited through custom. It's not a question that they have thought about it and have decided to trust it. *Nomizo*, this customary belief that is based on nothing other than the fact that it came from somewhere else, is not the word used for faith. The words for faith, believe and the verb 'to be persuaded', as you read through them in your Greek New Testament, all come from the same root verb. It means that you are sure that something is true and real so you know you can trust it. Which is why the Greeks never ever use the word *pistis* because the one thing they couldn't do was trust their gods.

Faith in the New Testament is inextricably linked with truth and reality. You can trust God because he is real and because he is true to his promises, to what he says. He is not inconsistent, he does not change his mind. How is it possible to have faith in God, even when horrible and terrible things befall you? Even though you don't know what is happening, you do know the One in whom everything is held together and you can trust him. That's why in Timothy 1:12, it doesn't say, 'I know what I have believed and I am convinced.' It says, 'I know whom I have believed, and am convinced.' Faith is not an intellectual speculation, faith is the only appropriate response to a God who is true and real. He is completely trustworthy and he is true to all of his promises.

We sometimes read those verses in the New Testament that say that even if we are faithless, God will be faithful and we read it as being reassurance. There's no reassurance there. That's not what's intended by that verse. If we are faithless, God will be faithful; to what? To whom? To himself. These are not threats, these are promises.

Christian certainty

We have every reason in this world to be certain. Christian certainty is not moral arrogance because we're not certain of ourselves, of our hearts or even of our own thoughts but we are certain of God. Faith is a gift because God has revealed himself. He has made himself known, he has taken the initiative, he has shown himself, through his word, through his world and latterly he has spoken to us by his Son. He has called us by his Spirit and we can trust him. We can have faith in him, even when we don't understand what is happening around us.

The world is uncertain of many things. Maybe we, as Christians, need to be less certain of some things which we hold and think are so certain. There's only one thing we can be certain of and that is God revealed to us in Christ. We can trust God because there is no moral failure in him. He is not like the Greek gods, who required custom, habit and law in order to produce belief. He is real and true. He is the subject of *pistis*; real faith, which is based on truth and reality. When difficult times come the more you know that God is real and the more you know that you can trust him, the more you will lean on him. As G.K. Chesterton said, 'The temptation can be, when things become difficult, to turn away from him but, in heaven's name, to what?' You can have faith in God in times of great uncertainty even in your own life, once you know that you can trust him and that God is real.

Keswick Lecture – Week 3

Total Mission
by Joseph D'Souza

JOSEPH D'SOUZA

Joseph D'Souza is President of the All India Christian Council, the largest inter-denominational alliance of Indian Christians worldwide. With more than two thousand constituent member bodies, the AICC has been at the forefront of the struggle for freedom of religion in India over the last seven years, since the onslaught of persecution against Christians began. Joseph has also been one of the main Christian voices for the emancipation of India's Dalits, who are breaking free from thousands of years of caste oppression, and he speaks on human rights and justice issues worldwide.

Total Mission

Introduction

What I'm going to share with you comes out of a long history in mission work and kingdom work within India, especially in the last seven years. When the persecution of Christians in India started about seven years ago, the Christian community in India was absolutely stunned. We'd always thought that a day might come when we would be persecuted, harassed and attacked but we never thought it would come the way it did and it would engage in the kind of activity it did. There was physical violence, there was hate propaganda against the Christian church and then there was anti-Christian legislation. Graham Staines' and his two sons' brutal killing informed the world that things were not right in India. But prior to that, for several years the persecution was on; it's on even today. It stunned the Indian Christians and it did some very good things. I've noticed that your theme for this Convention this year is the sovereignty of God. I've gone public among Christian circles and even non-Christian circles in India and around the world, and I say, 'I thank God for the persecution in India.' Because it did some very good and important things.

One, it brought us together as Christians, especially those who loved Jesus Christ, who loved what he had done for them on the cross and who were committed to carry that witness forward, in a hostile situation. And as we came together, we asked ourselves, 'How do we respond and how do we unite?' The question of unity forced us to come to the bare essentials of what is required for Christians to come together in the midst of crisis and persecution. And, to our utter delight, we found that it was very simple, not complicated. The simplicity was, we needed, all of us, who banded together, an uncompromising commitment to the uniqueness of Christ, who he was, what he had done on the cross. Our commitment was to stay true to that message. Because it was because of our faithful witness to Jesus Christ that we were being persecuted.

The second thing was, as we analysed, 'Why are they after us? Why this intensity of attack?' it became very clear that it was not primarily because of us but more because of a larger upheaval in the Indian nation among the oppressed caste of India, the Dalits. Two hundred and fifty million people have faced a religious-sanctioned racism for 3,000 years and even though the constitution bans discrimination, nothing, very little, has changed in larger Indian society. Those of you who are interested, have a look at this website: www.dalitnetwork.org

It became apparent to us that we were being attacked because the Dalits were in exodus from the Hindu caste system and a number of them were coming into the church. So we had to ask the question, quick and fast, 'What do we do? This attack is about forcing us to close the doors of our churches, the doors of our homes from the Dalits from entering in. Do we keep our doors open or do we close our doors?' We decided, if we were to be true to Jesus Christ, we had to keep our doors open and not only we had to keep our doors open, we had to go public and say, 'Like Jesus, him who comes to Jesus Christ, we will not shut out.' It was a momentous decision and a public decision. We did that and the word went out across the nation that there is a section, a very large section, of the Indian church that has gone on record that they will not close the doors of their church from the Dalits who want to enter in the kingdom of God and find salvation, deliverance, help in Jesus Christ.

Our analysis was exactly right. I remember soon after that, soon after the Graham Staines murder, being invited to Geneva, to a conference on minorities and human rights and requested to intervene on behalf of India. I spoke about the Indian persecution and I said, 'It is not about Christians, it was never about Christians but it was about the larger population outside.' That day we had a private meeting, with the then human rights commissioner, Mrs Mary Robinson. She had come back from a trip to India and when she was in India, the Government of India had given her their typical spin but she also had private meetings with lots of people. And she said, 'We agree with your thesis, it's not about Christians, it's about the Dalits.' So we said, 'We'll keep our door open.'

What followed surprised us, especially those of us who had been involved in mission and involved in seeing the kingdom of God and the kingdom of heaven extended in the land of India. The Dalit leaders turned back to us and said, 'You've gone public, will you join us now in our struggle for freedom? Your persecution of the Christian church for seven years,' (as of now: then, it was just a few years) 'is really a picnic, compared to what we have gone through for 3,000 years.'

Just in the year 2001, in the state of Uttar Pradesh, there were 25,000 barbaric, physical atrocities against the Dalits, which included burning of their homes, rape of their women, killing of innocent Dalits and the taking away of whatever little possessions they had. So here they come to us and say, 'Can you, the Christian church, join us in our struggle for freedom?' We said, 'Yes.'

What does that mean? Two things came up. The anti-conversion law in India has very little to do with present-day Christians in the church; it has everything to do with those who are outside and want to come in. For example, the law in Tamil Nadu, which has been repealed for the first time, identifies that the law is focused against Dalit tribals, women and children getting converted. The forces of right-wing Hinduism have not hidden their agenda, they're very clear.

So the Dalits ask us, 'Will you fight with us, for the larger fight, for freedom of conscience and freedom of religion and freedom of choice?' And we said, 'Yes we will.' Because this is biblical, this is kingdom. No man should be forced to give away the right to follow what his conscience is dictating. They've taken everything, now they want to take away even the freedom of conscience. We said, 'Yes, we will stand.'

'Secondly,' they said, 'will the Christian church let the worldwide community, especially the Christian community, know what has been done to us? Will you be in solidarity?' And we said, 'Yes, we will.'

Persecution began in '97, '98. I stand here before you to announce, with great encouragement – no arrogance, no conceit – I do not belong and do not want to be a party to any religious war, even being party of a Christian religious right party war, against other religions of the world. I have to make that position very clear but I have to announce that today tens of thousands of the Dalit people in the nation are finding Christ, freely, openly and coming in. This movement has not happened for the last 200 years. About a week ago, one of the groups that I'm associated with, on one day, in one place, baptised 675 people.

The resurgence of nationalism

This talk that I'm engaging in is based in a grass-root experience of the so-called two-thirds world church in India. As we address the subject of total mission, in the twenty-first millennium, it's important for us to understand, that the first decade of the twenty-first millennium has not exactly turned out to be the Utopian decade that Clinton and many political leaders promised before the new millennium dawned. I remember the speeches political leaders around the world gave. Glorious stories of globalisation, glorious stories of the breakdown of the Iron Curtain, stories that, somehow, peace would now descend on the world. Christians too, were caught up in that euphoria and they too believed that somehow, our mission context for the coming decades would change. We would have a more open, more welcoming mission context, around the world. Little did we know, that the tearing down of the Iron Curtain and the Communist empire would actually bring to the fore something that has been there for thousands of years within human history – cultural nationalism and religious nationalism. Would you have predicted in the year 1995, that in the year 2004 we would have a world that is more dominated by religious nationalism, rather than freedom, democracy, peace? Look at the world that we live in.

We have Islamic nationalism, getting stronger and stronger; purposeful, well co-ordinated, well planned. We have Hindu nationalism. In 1995, it was just emerging, out of its 60 year embryonic growth but nobody would have imagined it would be the monster it is today. And some would say today (I'm sorry, I know I'm in a Christian audience) that since the Iraq war, we now have the traces of a form of Christian nationalism. The world has become a very confused place for those of us who want to represent Jesus Christ, what he did on the cross and what the kingdom is all about.

We have problem number one: religious and cultural nationalism and it won't go that easily. We have a battle ahead of us.

Those of us who live in a context of religious nationalism, like India, and have tried to figure out 'How do we address it? How do we deal with it?' have been forced to look at church history and find answers. Not in recent Christian history, not even in reformation Christian history; we've had to go back to the early church and how it handled the early religious nationalism that was prevalent in the early centuries of the growth of the church.

Godless secularism

The second problem, the huge challenge that we have, is godless secularism: driven, dominated, instigated, created, I'm sorry again to say, by Europe. Legislation after legislation has been subtly brought that puts people of believing faith as outcasts, troublemakers, dissenters. The godless secularism of Europe has managed, through the state, to remove God not only out of public life, that is government life, but also out of social life. A great agenda to banish God out of human life altogether. How do we deal with this world? How do we bring the message, the good news of the kingdom of God and the kingdom of heaven, in a world that has removed God from the marketplace?

Post-Christian indifference

Thirdly, we have the huge challenge of post Christian disillusionment. In a number of places, when I have expanded on this subject, I have said that Paul had an advantage, the early apostles had an advantage that I don't have, that you don't have, the Christians of today don't have. I might even say, maybe, their job was easier. Why? They were preaching a new thing. There was no Christian faith, there was no Christian church. They were talking about God's kingdom, an ideal community, an ideal church that would be true to the teachings of Jesus Christ, true to the teachings of the Bible. People responded, believed, followed. But I live on the right side of that history, 2,000 years on and there is a history of Christianity, both good and bad. I have to deal with the issue of Christianity being linked with colonialism. I have to deal with the issue of Christianity being linked with apartheid. Today I have to deal with the issue of Christianity being linked with economic imperialism. My job and your job is tough and it calls for everything that I have, calls for everything that the church has, to respond to the challenge of our day. Why is it tough? It is tough because the issue is the credibility of Christianity. The Christian religion as an institution and Christianity are the credibility of Christians, themselves.

I have to add a qualifier to that. It has never been, and even today it has not ever been, a question of the credibility of Jesus Christ. That is a difference, a big difference: even the worst critics of the Christian church say, 'Jesus Christ was not like this.' So it's not the credibility of Jesus Christ but the credibility of, sometimes, what the church or Christians have engaged or linked themselves to. There are the good sides of the Christian church too but I face that problem in doing kingdom mission today.

Therefore the challenge is complex and it calls for total mission. I'm sorry to give you a new phrase; total mission, what kind of a phrase is that? I would love to use the words incarnate mission and I'm going to refer to that. That's the best words but every phrase I've tried has been hijacked by somebody for their own purposes. For example, I would like to say, 'What I'm talking about today is the full gospel.' That's been hijacked. I would like to say, 'What I'm talking about today is holistic.' But holistic, often, means doing good, compassionate work but doesn't encompass the whole thing. What I'm talking about is modelling our mission according to Jesus, incarnate and total. For that to be expanded and understood, I need to look at a few texts. Would you turn with me to some very familiar texts in the gospel of Matthew.

The Great Commission

Look at chapter 28:18. The two critical parts of the Great Commission are the call to make disciples and how Jesus said we should make disciples: both are here. '… go and make disciples of all nations'. How do they do it? Verse 20, '… teaching them to obey everything I have commanded you.'

May I suggest to you that in the last couple of decades especially, in the worldwide global mission movement, there has been a form of gospel reductionism. We have removed the aspects of the gospels we don't like, that disturb us, and the gospel has been reduced to its barest minimum. For many people, all that it means is a ticket to heaven, nothing else. Here, Jesus does not give me that luxury. He tells me that if I'm going to go and do the Great Commission, I have to make disciples and I have to teach them all things. Not some things, not a few things, not the most common, bare minimum denominator. I have to teach them all things. And the all things that Jesus is referring to are the all things of the kingdom of God and the kingdom of heaven and life in obedience to God, that he taught in the gospels; all things. But remember, he doesn't stop there. He says 'teach them' so there is the cognitive aspect, the understanding aspect, but he goes further, 'teach them to obey'.

That's a very difficult job. 'Teach them to practise everything that I have taught you.' It doesn't say teach them to go and get a PhD on the kingdom of God, according to Jesus Christ. No, he says, 'teach them to practise'. And how do you teach anybody to practise, if you and I, like Jesus Christ, don't model that obedience? Here is a secret. Do we want to deal with the credibility issue of the Christian faith? Do we want to deal with godless secularism? Do we want to deal with religious nationalism? Here is a secret: model, practise, live out the kingdom of God and teach those who are coming in, to practise the kingdom teachings. It's a tall, tall order but it is possible to the Holy Spirit, possible by God's grace, to teach people to be a new kind of people.

Turn to Matthew 23. There was a false religion and a false practice, during Jesus' time, which he challenged; the practice of the Pharisees. Look at verse 13, where he says, 'Woe to you, teachers of the law and Pharisees, you hypocrites! You shut the kingdom of heaven in men's faces. You yourselves do not enter, nor will you let those enter who are trying to.'

This is one of the most serious statements Jesus made, about the power of religious leaders. Not only within the Jewish system, I believe in all systems. Those of us who know the history of Europe and the Reformation, know what the power of religious leaders is and how Martin Luther, Wycliffe, Knox, Calvin had to break free. Awesome power.

Problem, verse 23, 'Woe to you, teachers of the law and Pharisees, you hypocrites! You give a tenth of your spices – mint, dill and cummin. But you have neglected the more important matters of the law – justice, mercy and faithfulness. You should have practised the latter, without neglecting the former. You blind guides! You strain out a gnat but swallow a camel.' Very strong words, 'You're great at the small peripheral things, of dotting i's and crossing the t's. You're great in determining external behaviour and all kinds of regulations, but you missed the point. You neglect the call of true religion; the struggle for justice and righteousness, the application of mercy on this earth. Faithfulness towards God, that's not there.' What a condemnation of a false religion and what a challenge to us.

The three ways to do mission

There are three ways we can do mission, in our present context, as we have outlined what the challenges are.

The incarnate way

We can do it the incarnate way, the total way. What is the total way? You remain within society, you go to the heart of society, you take on the challenges of the society and you work out the kingdom of God, the good news, at the heart of society. You deal with the main issues that the kingdom of God and the Bible wants us to deal with. Articulate the spirituality that comes because of grace, that takes justice and righteousness seriously, that gives a high value on being faithful to God and having a different lifestyle.

The mission compound model

Or if you don't want to do incarnate mission, you can have another model; stay outside the world, have nothing to do there, evangelise, throw some bullets, bombs and hope you can pull some people out. That's been done and history has shown, in the long run, that does not transform society, that does not extend the kingdom of God. In India we have examples, in the last 200 years, of what has been called mission compound Christianity. There was so-called evangelisation, people were converted, brought out and then we created our own little mission compound, our own little ghetto. And finally, at the end, a few decades later, the people weren't part of India, nor were they part of the Christian faith. They never had to deal with the tough issues of spiritual life, of discipleship. What does it mean to be a disciple in the marketplace? If I'm in finance, what does it mean to be a disciple in the finance world? If I'm in the arts, what does it mean to be a disciple in the art world?

That's one of the sad models of mission that was brought to our country. I have to suggest to you it was because of a sad, inadequate, incomplete kind of Christianity that existed in the west. A Christian church that lived at the margins took a gospel that also was living at the margins. A Christian church that had failed to tackle society as a whole took a gospel that also taught the nationals how not to tackle society as a whole. We can only take what we do and what we are. We cannot take and do what we are not.

The challenge for today is to review, rethink and say, Jesus did not only become man, he became a Jew, he came within a Jewish culture. Yes, he came to die for our sins but look at all that he did. He challenged the evil of his day, the religious structure of his day. Would he have been killed if his mouth was shut about the false religion that was being practised in his day? I don't believe he would have been killed but he spoke out. He became a public figure. On the one hand, he gave good news and drew the sinners, the prostitutes, the tax collectors to him. On the other hand, he took on evil.

What Jesus did on the cross

I need to look at the two-fold work of the cross, in Colossians 2:13–15. What a glorious description. He dealt with the sin problem. But it does not stop there; he also dealt with the problem of evil, on this earth and in the earth beyond, in the heavens and the world beyond. The cross is always about two things; death to sin, death to evil; death to sin, death to Satan. To only think of personal sin and forget evil, forget Satan, forget the demonic forces and how they work in the world and not to understand what the cross did to that evil is to have only half the gospel. We need both and the forces of the cross that are at work today are dealing with both the problems: the sin and the problem of evil. Christians sometimes like to stay in closeted rooms and closeted churches where they're quite happy to deal with issues of personal sin but they don't want, like Jesus, to go out there and to challenge evil, to raise their voices.

I know about a year and a half ago, here in Britain, a big music label took two girls from the former Soviet Union and they brought out a pop song, which for the first time on MTV marketed lesbianism in song. The band's name was Tatou. And there was a cry from many women's groups, here in Britain. My question is, where was the human cry of the Christian church?

Being involved in the quest for justice and righteousness does mean taking up the offence, in compassion, in mercy, in gladness, without arrogance, raising up our voice. There is a greater evil that's going on, that not only damns those who don't know the gospel but also affects our own children who are out there. Their spiritual destinies are being affected by that evil. I'm not only talking about India, I'm also talking about Britain and godless secularism.

What is total mission? It is the good news of Jesus Christ. Kingdom mission is the good news of Jesus Christ, the announcement of the good news of Jesus Christ, of what he has done on the cross.

As Paul said, 'the gospel is the power of God.' It's not just theory, it does something to people. The gospel is loving service, it is *koinonia*, it is compassionate service. The gospel is also a community, a new kind of community, a new kind of people. That's the challenge you and I have today.

I have to remind us of one of the biggest challenges that was raised to the Indian church and the global church about fifty years ago by a man called Dr B.R. Ambedkar. When he wanted to look at different options for his people, the Dalits, one reason he rejected Christianity was because we did not display community and *koinonia*. He said, 'My people, who have been divided into 2,000 sub groups, need a religion that brings them together, gives them equality but unites them, creates a new equal community but also a united community. When I look at the Indian church in India, I find they divide my people. If there is a movement among the Dalits, then there will be 20 denominations, who go among a 1,000 people group and divide them into 20 groups. Somebody believes in this Bible and he goes and forms a church, somebody believes in this translation of the Bible, he goes and forms another church.' He said, 'My India does not need any more fragmentation. The Brahmins have fragmented our people enough.'

Isn't the gospel and the new community, the church, about unity? Isn't it about creating a new humanity, that is no male, no female, no Greek, no Jew, no rich, no poor, no slave, bringing all of us together? That's the gospel, that's mission, that's what we are called to do. Kingdom mission also is about crisis, the Hebrew word, the thirst for justice and righteousness and working for it and we've had some glorious examples in the church of Christ.

My all-time great hero is William Carey. I've heard some missiologists criticise William Carey because, 'In his whole life,' they say, 'he brought only three people to Christ.' That is the criticism. That's a very bad and wrong way of evaluating William Carey's work. It's William Carey's work that has opened the doors for us today. I don't know from where he got his wisdom. For me, it's a mystery, he must have been a genius of enormous proportions. He went into India and he saw *suttee* and he saw child marriage and he campaigned against it. He campaigned against it within the system, he campaigned against it with his British rulers and he worked and worked and worked, until *suttee* was ultimately banished and child marriage was outlawed. Today's Hindus are trying to bring *suttee* back. You and I will not know till we go to heaven, how many Indian women came to Christ because of that one act of caring. He stood for what the Bible is all about and righteousness is all about and the quest for justice is all about.

My challenge to you today is, as you think of mission, think of the call for being salt and light. Think, what does Britain need? Think, are words only enough? Think, hasn't the time come for, whatever size the evangelical community in Britain is, to get out of their churches and find God's place, where he's at work, trying to do something new and play your part in it?

The Addresses

The Calling of the First Disciples

Matthew 4:18–22

by Anne Graham Lotz

ANNE GRAHAM LOTZ

Anne Graham Lotz was born and reared in Montreat, North Carolina, the second daughter of Billy and Ruth Graham. She is the wife of Dr Dan Lotz and the mother of three children. From 1976–88 Anne taught Bible Study Fellowship, a weekly Bible study class in Raleigh, North Carolina, of over five hundred women. Her original class multiplied until today there are ten other classes of similar size in Raleigh. In 1988, Anne established AnGeL Ministries, a non-profit corporation, which seeks to give out messages of biblical exposition through her speaking, tapes and books. Her first book *The Vision of His Glory* and her second book *God's Story* both won the Gold Medallion Awards. Anne was the only woman to be a plenary speaker at the International Congress of Itinerant Evangelists in Amsterdam in 1983 and 1986, at the School of Evangelism in Moscow in 1991, and at the Global Christian Workers Conference from San Juan, Puerto Rico in 1995. She also serves on the Board of Directors for the Billy Graham Evangelistic Association and the Evangelical Council of Financial Accountability. Anne's aim is clear – it is to bring revival to the heart of God's people. And her message is consistent – she calls people to a personal relationship with God through his word.

The Calling of the First Disciples
Matthew 4:18–22

Introduction

Jesus Christ, in a world that is out of control, is God to the rescue. My message for you is a challenge to take that thrill and maintain it every day for the rest of your lives. The joy of the Lord is our strength and as we go out into a joyless world, it is the joy in knowing Jesus and making him known that is contagious to the world. They want to know our God because they see us enjoying him, yet it can be so easy somehow to lose that joy.

I think our joy in Jesus is directly related to our focus. Sometimes you talk to the person next to you and think, I have never met someone so mature in their faith, and it makes you feel small. Or maybe you think, I can't believe such an immature person would be here, and you feel very superior. Or maybe you are in ministry and you talked to somebody and you found out that they're in ministry and their church is taking off. In your church you can barely get people to come to a Bible reading or prayer meeting and you can feel so depressed. If we are not careful we are going to lose our joy because we are comparing ourselves with each other.

My challenge to you is to work at maintaining your focus on Jesus that you might maintain your joy in knowing him and making him known every day of your life. My theme is from Matthew 3 and 4 but the text I would like to draw is from 1 Peter chapter 1. Peter served the Lord for three years, then witnessed the cross, the resurrection, the ascension and Pentecost. Then he became a preacher and evangelist and he opened the door for the gospel to go to the Gentiles and then we lost track of him, but the last year of his life he writes this letter and in the last year of Peter's life, he would say, 'I have known Jesus almost all of my life and because of my relationship with Jesus I have been beaten, imprisoned, persecuted, falsely accused but I am here to tell you, at the end of my life, I am still thrilled to know Jesus Christ. I still have the joy of knowing him and making him known.' 'Peter, how have you been able to do that knowing of the imprisonments, beatings and persecutions? How can you maintain the joy in your discipleship?'

The grace of God

Chosen by the Father

Peter answers from his letter, chapter 1:1–12. Peter, all of his life, has maintained his focus. First of all, he has maintained his focus on the grace of God in his life (verses 1,2) Peter can never get over the joy of the thrill of God's grace; the fact that he was chosen by the Father, changed by the Spirit and cleansed by the Son. I was chosen by the Father to be a disciple of the Son and I have never got over the thrill. Out of all the people in Galilee, all the people living on planet Earth, why would God say 'Peter, I want you to belong to my Son'? That's God's grace.

Changed by the Spirit

Peter was not only chosen by the Father but he was being changed by the Spirit (verse 2). This was especially meaningful because Peter failed so dramatically and publicly. I think Gethsemane was probably the most dramatic failure, when Jesus asked Peter to pray with him and Peter went to sleep. And can you imagine what it would have been like to be Peter and to know that the last thing your Lord heard you say before he went to the cross was 'I don't know him'? Peter must have wept tears of bitterness and regret: 'If only I could take that back.' But he couldn't. Peter was such a failure.

Have you ever failed? I was in an audience once when Dr Alan Redpath was preaching and he asked, 'Do you know what God expects of you? All God ever expects of you is failure.' I was so startled and thought, I can do that. I can live up to the expectations of God. Then Alan Redpath said, 'But he has given you the Holy Spirit so that you need never fail', and I thought, That's it, living a life of victory is living a life in the Spirit. I learned to yield my life to him so that I surrender to the moment by moment control of the Holy Spirit and as I do that, the Holy Spirit within me transforms me and sanctifies me so that increasingly I become like Jesus. Peter failed and failed and failed again – he was so grateful for God's grace that had given him the Spirit of Jesus to live inside of him that anything God required of Peter would be called out from the Spirit within him. It wasn't up to Peter on his own to live a life of discipleship, it was up to Peter to yield his life to the Holy Spirit and the Holy Spirit would live the life of Christ through him. And Peter learned to yield his life to the Holy Spirit and he was increasingly sanctified. Peter would tell you, 'Keep your focus on the grace of God who has given you the person of the Holy Spirit.' The Holy Spirit is Jesus living inside of you and will enable, equip and empower you to be a disciple. Peter was so grateful that he was being changed into the image of Christ by the Holy Spirit and that is God's grace.

Cleansed by the Son

Thirdly, he was grateful that he was being continually cleansed by the Son, sprinkled by the blood of Jesus. Jesus said to Peter, 'Who do people say that I am?' and Peter said 'Some people say you're Jeremiah, some say you're Isaiah, even John the Baptist come back from the dead.' Jesus said, 'Peter, who do you say that I am?' Peter looked at Jesus and said, 'I believe that you are the Christ, the Messiah, God walking the Earth in a human body, the incarnation of God himself.' Jesus said, 'Peter, God has revealed that to you, you are right.' Then Jesus confided in Peter and said, 'I am going to a cross' and Peter said, 'No you're not.' Jesus rebuked Peter because Satan was speaking through him. And Peter discovered that the cross was necessary. If for no one else, it was necessary for him because he was a sinner, a failure and Peter had to come to the cross and receive forgiveness and he knew what it was like to live in his forgiveness. Peter still sinned and had to come back to the cross, to be cleansed that he might maintain his fellowship with the Father, the Son and the Spirit.

When you come to the cross initially for salvation and you confess your sin, all of your sin is forgiven. Did you know that? The cross was 2,000 years ago so when you confess your sin, that cross applies to all of your sin, past sin, present and future because it was all future at that point. When Jesus died, he died for all of your sin – big ones, little ones and medium-sized ones; past and present and future – it's all forgiven. You will never come under the judgement of God, ever, for your sins, because Jesus has paid it all. He took the judgement in your place on the cross. I tell you what, that is something to shout about, isn't it? Praise God. But you and I still sin.

When you are aware that you have sinned and had that ugly thought or snapped back at somebody or told a lie or had a jealous attitude, you come to the cross by faith and say 'God, I'm sorry' and you name your sin for what it is. Don't play games with the labels – you know, sometimes I lie and I call it exaggeration or I don't believe God and I call it worry and we can switch the labels and make it seem less like sin but 1 John 1:9 says you confess your sin – you say the same thing about it God does, you call it what he calls it. And when you do, then he cleanses you from every sin and all sins and you have to be cleansed in order to maintain your fellowship with the Father. When you come to the cross initially, you are forgiven of all your sins – praise God we are forgiven. But we come back to the cross every day for cleansing so that we might be in right fellowship with God and maintain the sweetness of our relationship with him. Peter was such a failure and even after Pentecost, he still made mistakes and he was so grateful that he was continually cleansed by the blood of Jesus.

When was the last time you went to the cross? Was it for your salvation, when you were converted? Every day we come back to the cross and claim the blood of Jesus to cleanse us from any and all sin that we might maintain our fellowship with the Father. If you don't do that, sin in your life that is not confessed is a joy-robber and you will lose the joy of knowing Jesus. You've been chosen by the Father to be a disciple of the Son. You are being changed and conformed into the image of Jesus by the Spirit of Jesus who lives in you. And you are constantly being cleansed by his blood as you come and confess your sin. If you want to maintain the joy of knowing Jesus and the joy of making him known, then keep your focus on God's grace in your lives.

God's gifts

The hope of the resurrection

Secondly, Peter kept his focus on God's gifts in his life and at the end of his life, Peter was primarily preoccupied with two gifts and the first one was the living hope of the resurrection (versus 3). This was especially meaningful to Peter because he would never forget he had denied his Lord and witnessed the crucifixion and Jesus had died. And he thought Jesus was the Messiah. Peter must have gone into shock for three days, barricaded in that upper room, in grief and turmoil. Early Sunday morning, he heard someone banging on the door and it was Mary and she was saying something about the tomb being empty. Peter and John ran through Jerusalem and came to the tomb and the stone was rolled away. Peter charged inside that tomb and he looked around in a rage because the tomb was empty and he saw the grave clothes lying there but that didn't make sense. And when the women came to the tomb, Jesus met them and said 'Go, tell my disciples and Peter that I have risen from the dead.'

Later, the disciples on the road to Emmaus, after Jesus had revealed himself to them, ran all the way back to Jerusalem and said, 'We've seen the Lord. He has appeared to us and to Peter.' Somewhere in between those two encounters, Peter had an encounter with the risen Lord Jesus Christ. Peter, who knew that our Lord's ears must have been ringing with his denial as he went to the cross, saw the arms of Jesus opened wide and knew Jesus had died for him and his sins were forgiven. He came into the living hope of the resurrection: failure isn't final. Our God is a God of a second chance and a third chance and fourth.

Later, beside the Sea of Galilee, Peter had been fishing all night and Jesus called him and Peter realised it was Jesus and plunged out of the boat, running to Jesus because he wanted him back in his life so desperately. Jesus fixed him breakfast and beside the fire – Peter had been beside a fire when he denied our Lord and now beside a fire once again – Peter confesses his love for Jesus where three times before he had denied his Lord and Peter was restored. He writes in his letter, 'to those of us who believe he is so precious.' Peter knew what it was to come into the living hope of the resurrection, to know his sins were forgiven, that he was accepted by God, that failure doesn't have to be final, that God would give him another chance, God could use him as a disciple.

I think the cross was the worst thing Peter had ever seen. Actually the cross is the worst thing anyone has ever seen. Some of you perhaps chose not to see Mel Gibson's movie. I saw it as a preview and I came away wondering, was it that bad and then thinking, Isaiah said that he was marred more than any man, it had to be worse than even that film revealed. If God could bring the resurrection, the glory and the redemption of humankind and our salvation from something as wretched and horrible as the cross, what do you think he can do with the mess that you have made in your lives? The living hope of the resurrection is this – God can bring blessing from brokenness, life from death, glory from the grave. Whatever it is in your life that has got you so down, bring it to Jesus and experience the living hope of the resurrection.

There's a wonderful story. Some fishermen in the highlands of Scotland had been fishing all day and they came into the pub at night to order their drinks. While the waitress was getting their drinks they were telling the stories about the fish that got away and one fisherman was describing the size of the fish that got away and he threw out his arms just when the maid was bringing the tray of drinks. His hand hit the tray and the drinks smashed up against the whitewashed wall and everybody was staring at this ugly brown stain that immediately developed on this whitewashed wall. Before they could move, a man in the corner jumped up and pulled out of his pocket a piece of charcoal and began to sketch around the ugly brown stain and it was transformed into a magnificent stag running across a highland meadow. His name was Sir Edwin Landseer. He was one of Great Britain's foremost wildlife artists. The lesson is that it was an ugly brown stain until a master artist took hold of it and turned it into a masterpiece. What's the ugly brown stain in your life? Every day you are reminded of that choice – would you surrender it to Jesus? The Master can take that ugly brown stain and bring something glorious out of it. That's the living hope of the resurrection. Peter was so grateful as he focused on God at the end of his life and, of course, the living hope of the resurrection meant that one day Peter, in his flesh, would see God. This life is not all there is.

The lasting inheritance

The second gift he was thinking about was that lasting inheritance that he would have (verse 4). Peter was aware that God was reserving an inheritance for him in heaven, that one day Peter would go and claim it, just like that song says that one day we are 'boldly going to approach the throne and claim the crown in Christ alone.' Jesus says 'Don't let your heart be troubled, don't be afraid; believe in God, believe also in me. In my Father's house there is room for everybody and I'm going to go ahead and prepare it for you.' Jesus has been preparing this place for 2,000 years.

As I sat on the hillside out on Honister Pass, I thought how beautiful everything is around here. God has created this beauty –

what has he thought of for heaven? How glorious it's going to be – he knows the colours that I like and he knows the landscape that I enjoy and he knows the music I want to hear and the friends I want to see and he's preparing it for me and preparing a place for you and one day, Revelation 21 says, God himself is going to welcome you into my Father's house and he's going to wipe the tears from your face and there'll be no more suffering and no more pain. You have an inheritance that's lasting, laid up for you in heaven so don't get out of focus. Sometimes we think, God, if I'm your child and you bless me then why can't I have that? I see these wicked people with all these things and the Lord tells me, 'Wait till you come home and see what I'm preparing for you.'

Our precious mother can't walk any more, she has a difficult time speaking, she has macular degeneration so she can't read her Bible any more and she has a little illustration she uses about herself. My parents live in a very old log cabin and they have lots of mice and my mother used to set traps for the mice but when a mouse gets in a trap, the trap can squash the mouse and be messy. So mother came up with these glueboards and she puts peanut butter in the middle of it and the mouse crawls to get the peanut butter, gets stuck on the glueboard and you can pick up the whole board and throw it away. My precious mother says, 'Anne, I'm like a mouse stuck on a glueboard' because she can't get up by herself and she can't get down by herself and she can't feed herself and she can't clothe herself and she's totally helpless, like a little mouse stuck on a glueboard.

The last time I was over, I said, 'Mother, how is it? You are a mouse stuck on a glueboard, but your eyes always twinkle, you're always full of life, you always know where I am, what's going on, you're interested in everything and how is it that you're so filled with joy?' She said, 'Anne, I have so much to look forward to.' Looking forward to her lasting inheritance laid up in heaven because she also has a living hope of the resurrection. She knows this life is not all there is and she is living for her inheritance.

Keep your focus

Times of trial

Peter, at the end of his life, maintained the joy in knowing Jesus and making him known because he kept his focus on God's grace and on God's gift and on God's glory. He tells us in verses 6, 7 'In this you greatly rejoice, though now for a little while you may have had to suffer grief in all kinds of trials. These have come so that your faith – of greater worth than gold, which perishes even though refined by fire – may be proved genuine and may result in praise, glory and honour when Jesus Christ is revealed.' The thrill stayed with Peter all of his life. Peter is saying, 'The glory of God can be revealed in my life and other people can look at me and see Jesus.' Do you know when this takes place the most dramatically? It's when you suffer grief and all kinds of trials.

A couple of years ago I went to see the crown jewels at the Tower of London. They are absolutely spectacular, diamonds as big as golf balls, and emeralds as big as goose eggs and they sparkle like they are on fire. They are laid on black velvet and the jewels are spectacular but it's the black velvet that shows off the glory of the jewels. The trials and sufferings and pressures in our lives are the black velvet and God lets them come into our lives so that other people can look at us and see the contrast of the glory of the character of Jesus in us against our sufferings.

If you have all the money you want in the bank and your hair's always perfect, your body is in good shape, your children always behave, your health is perfectly in order, your business is going wonderfully, and you're kind and thoughtful and you tell people about Jesus – they're going to shrug: 'If I'd a life like that, I could be nice too.' But when your spouse has walked out on you, your child has been killed in an accident, you've been diagnosed with a disease and things are going wrong and everything is crashing in and then you're kind and you have peace in your heart and there's joy on your face – people sit up and take notice because they know that's not natural – that's supernatural. They can see the glory of God in your life. Peter says rejoice when you have trials because the trials are the black velvet, they come so that your faith would shine through, your faith would prove genuine.

At times when I have felt abandoned in the last few years, I have turned to Hebrews and God says, 'I will never leave you, I will never forsake you.' I might feel abandoned but my faith doesn't rest on my feelings, my faith rests on the word of God. You put your faith in the word of God, not your feelings, your circumstances and it's proved genuine when your circumstances are crashing all around you. You stand rock solid because your faith is in his word. Verse 8, 'Though you have not seen him, you love him' and when you are going through these trials you love him and are not offended with him and what he has allowed in your life, you trust him. In verse 8, he says, … 'you believe in him and are filled with an inexpressible and glorious joy' right in the midst of your suffering. Your joy is in Jesus, in knowing him and making him known. You know that whatever happens in your life is for a greater purpose and God is working out all things together for your good and his glory. Romans 8:28 says that all things work together for your good and sometimes we think our good is our health and wealth and prosperity and we think, God, you haven't kept your promise because all things are not good in my life – that's not what he means. For you and me, the ultimate good is that we be conformed to the image of Christ. That means when I am in his will and am called according to his purpose, everything that comes into my life, he allows for the purpose of conforming me to the image of Christ. So not only are these hardships and sufferings revealing the glory of God through me to others but they are constantly working, like pressure in my life, to conform and mould me into the image of Jesus. So we can rejoice that, in the midst of our suffering, what you and I have, the rest of the world hasn't. Our suffering isn't wasted, God will use it for his own glory to conform us to his image and to reveal himself to the world around us. That's his grace. Keep your focus on God's grace and his gift and his glory.

Focus on the gospel

Lastly, keep your focus on his gospel (verse 10). In the Old Testament, the gospel was just a promise – think about Adam and Eve after they had sinned and paradise was lost and they were coming under God's judgement – God gave them a promise and he said one day there will come a seed of a woman who will take away your sin and bring you back into a right relationship with your Creator and right then and there, Adam and Eve began to look for and long for the gospel. They didn't understand it, they didn't know the details but they knew that God had given them a promise that a seed would redeem them from their sin.

Then we come to Abraham, living in Ur. God says: 'Abraham, if you will follow me in a life of faith I will give you a seed' and Galatians says that was singular. Abraham knew, according to Paul in Galatians, that God was promising a Deliverer, a Redeemer. He was promising the gospel that would come through Abraham's line and Abraham longed for and looked for the gospel. He didn't know the details and he didn't know the name of Jesus, it was just a promise to him.

And in Deuteronomy God said, 'Moses, I am going to raise up a Deliverer like you but he is not going to deliver my people from bondage to slavery, he will deliver my people from bondage to sin.' Moses looked for and longed for the gospel. Isaiah was promised a lamb by whose stripes he would be healed and he didn't know the details but he longed for the gospel.

In the Old Testament, the gospel was a promise and they claimed it when they came to the Temple and grasped the lamb and confessed their sin and killed the lamb and the blood was sprinkled on the altar and they walked away knowing the blood of bulls and goats doesn't take away sin but they did it by faith looking forward to the cross that they did not understand. It was just a promise. Praise God we live on this side on the cross. I don't have to go to the Temple and sacrifice. I can look back to the cross and know the name of my Saviour. And we know his name – it's not a promise any more, it's a possession. We can claim it for ourselves and proclaim it.

When was the last time you told somebody who does not know Jesus about Jesus? Has it been a long time? That may be why you have lost the joy of knowing Jesus. There is nothing more thrilling than when you share Christ with somebody. They might not receive Christ at that moment but you have planted a seed and at some point that person will come to faith and maybe God will give you the privilege of being the person who is there when the last seed is sown and they place their faith in Jesus. And if you leave it up to the professionals then you avoid that responsibility and you are going to lose joy. God's given you and me that privilege and it's to be a blessing to us because there is so much joy to be received when we share Jesus with other people. So tell other people about him and that is one way that you maintain your focus on Jesus. In a world out of control, Jesus is God to the rescue.

It's not how we begin our life of discipleship that is important, it's how we end and when we stand before God we want to give an account of our life. I know we have made mistakes and sinned and failed and taken some wrong turns but from this day forward, can we agree together that we would choose to maintain our focus on Jesus that we might enjoy knowing him in a personal, permanent, love relationship and that we might enjoy making him known. Stay focused on his grace in your life, on his gift, his glory especially when the bad things come. Stay focused on his gospel as you tell the whole world that God loves them and that Jesus saves.

The Sermon on the Mount

Matthew 5–7

by Steve Brady

STEVE BRADY

Steve was converted in his teens in Liverpool and trained at London Bible College, during which time he met and married Brenda. They have two children, Paul and Ruth and a grandson, Daniel. Steve held pastorates in Leicester, London and Bournemouth before becoming Principal of Moorlands College, which trains men and women for Christian service at home and overseas. His preaching has taken him to conferences and conventions throughout the UK and abroad. Steve serves on the Councils of the Evangelical Alliance and the Keswick Convention and is a member of the Tyndale Fellowship. He's a keen sportsman and hates gardening!

The Sermon on the Mount

Matthew 5–7

Introduction

I would like you to turn with me to Matthew 5–7. We are going to read some very familiar words from the so-called Sermon on the Mount, from Matthew 5:1-12; 7:28,29.

For nearly five long years, Europe had lain under the tyranny and terror of Nazi Germany. But in a certain location down in Hampshire, at HMS Dryad, Admiral Ramsay and Generals Montgomery and Eisenhower were waiting. There had been so much covert preparation and suddenly the day dawned – 5 June 1944 – just over sixty years ago. But the weather was atrocious and the longed-for liberation of Europe was put on hold. And then there was a change and the weather forecasters said this was the time – 6 June 1944. General Eisenhower uttered two words that changed the face of Europe and all of subsequent history: 'Let's go.' Within hours, men and machines in their thousands, and within days in their tens of thousands, were pouring onto the Normandy beaches as the liberation of Europe began.

For millennia, the human race lay under a tyranny far worse than anything the Nazis could concoct: a nightmare of evil in God's world and wickedness in the human heart. On earth, here and there, were little pockets of light and hope and promise. Then, marvellously, 'when the time had fully come' (Gal. 4:4), the Triune God said, 'Let's go.' Firstly, in the womb of the virgin, and then in the manger at Bethlehem, the Son of God commences the greatest invasion of all time. We live on a planet that is one of nine planets that goes around a seemingly obscure sun. Out there in our galaxy, the Milky Way, there are perhaps a hundred billion similar suns. And in our universe there are maybe two billion similar galaxies. So there are potentially zillions of planets in the 'known' universe (who really knows – see Psalm 147:4?) Why is this planet significant? Why does it matter? Because it was to this world, dark, defiant and incommunicado with its Maker, that the eternal Son of God personally came to commence the great invasion and effect the great rescue.

Matthew has hinted at all this already in his gospel. In chapter 1, he introduces the genealogy of Jesus, the rightful heir to the throne of David, and the longed-for long-promised Messiah. Then he used a phrase through which he expects us to see prismatically all that is in the gospel: 'You shall call his name Jesus, for he shall save his people from their sins' (1:21). What is our greatest need? It is to be rescued from our sins. But who can do that?

Chapter 1:23 has the answer to our need: the One who bears the name 'Immanuel.' Not just 'God *is* with us', as he is with us tonight in a spiritual and general sense. No, the way Matthew expresses it is clear: it is 'God with us', literally God himself. And then Matthew proceeds to add to this Jesus, the Christ and Immanuel. He is the 'king of the Jews' (2:2), the Father's beloved Son (3:17). Even the devil knows his identity, 'the Son of God' (4:3).

Before Matthew has finished his gospel, he will have added all sorts of other titles: that mysterious and elusive phrase Jesus often used 'The Son of Man' ; the 'Servant of the Lord' who delivers what all the other servants only dimly could do; he is 'Lord' – the sufficient Christ. There are other titles we could add. Why? Because this One who comes to our rescue stands unique and supreme in a class all of his own. Eduard Schweizer, a New Testament scholar, puts it this way, 'He is the man who fits no formula.' He's not like anybody else, he is the man who fits no formula because uniquely he is the God-Man. And the King who comes to rescue us declares in his Sermon on the Mount manifesto just how the subjects of his kingdom are to live.

Now there are three things about Jesus, as we come to this Sermon, that we need to hold tightly onto or we will misinterpret his words completely.

First, this Jesus is supremely the *Redeemer:* he saves his people from their sins. Secondly, he is the *Revealer*: he is the One who makes the Father known – read all about that towards the end of chapter 11. As John's gospel states it: '[He] who has seen me, has seen the Father' (14:9). Thirdly, he is the *Renewer*. He will talk later on in the gospel about 'the renewal of all things' (19:28). There is coming a better day, Jesus promises, for this world. There is a whole new universe coming, 'a new heaven and a new earth, the home of righteousness' (2 Pet. 3:13). And all that glorious future is inextricably linked to Jesus – he literally is the future.

What's all this got to do with the Sermon on the Mount?

Everything! You see, one of our great dangers, when we approach this Sermon, is to lift out the sayings of Jesus as if they stand alone. At the moment, I am just reviewing a new translation of the New Testament, *Good as New*. I need to say loud and long and strong, for various reasons, I do not recommend it. For instance, the translator dumps eight New Testament books including the last one, Revelation, finding the latter unchristian! But he interestingly adds what he believes to be a 'fifth gospel', the so-called gospel of Thomas. It's one of a collection now termed the Gnostic gospels, and written, at the earliest, around the mid-second century AD. It's become fairly popular with some radical New Testament scholars. So why not include it in our Bibles? Simple – the gospel of Thomas is no gospel at all. It is a collection of purported sayings of Jesus. But there is no story-line about the life, death and resurrection of Jesus.

Here is the mistake we can so easily make with this Sermon. Of course, Jesus is the Revealer. He speaks and teaches like no one else. He is the truth of God incarnate. But it is not simply by what he says that we are saved but the whole package of who he is, God the Rescuer, and what he came to do when he died for us on the cross. So the Sermon must be read in the light of the whole gospel of Matthew. Otherwise, you have a Sermon without a Saviour. You've got principles but no power. You've grabbed a manifesto of ethics without an Energiser to make them possible.

So what does the King announce in his kingdom manifesto? What does it look like when he reigns over his subjects? How do people change when they bow to his authority, obey his teaching and manifest his wisdom in their lives? I propose three questions to guide us through these three chapters in Matthew.

Is this sermon reliable?

Here is the first question we want to ask of this Sermon. Can we trust it, is it reliable? I have mentioned the Gospel of Thomas. There is a self-appointed group of scholars in America called the Jesus Seminar. They vote on what bits of the sayings of Jesus they think are reliable. Not all of this Sermon makes the cut, so far as they are concerned. In addition, there is a runaway bestseller – it's sold over twelve million copies – by Dan Brown, a piece of fiction called *The Da Vinci Code*. If you read it, you may find all sorts of doubts being subtly sown in your mind about the Christian faith: how, in the fourth century, the Christian church came to prominence and power under Constantine and then used their position to suppress all their opponents who had what we now call these Gnostic gospels, and so got rid of an alternative version of Jesus. Talk about a rewriting of history! The book, dangerously, is a good read! If you don't know your Bible, your history and what other reputable scholars really think about the integrity of the New Testament and this Sermon, you can feel all at sea.

Thankfully, there is another side to the story. Let me suggest two or three things to help us.

According to tradition, this gospel was written by Matthew. Who was he? A tax collector. What would he do? I know, collect taxes!

How would he know who had to pay what? By keeping records, of course. To do that, he would have to develop and maintain an eye for detail. He would be used to jotting things down, making notes and following things up in detail later. Do you think that might have come in handy as he followed Jesus around? Do you think, given his training and experience, he might just have made some notes on that marvellous teaching which day after day, over a three-year period, he was hearing? Personally, I never listen to anybody speak without making notes because memory has been defined as that faculty by which we forget things. Do you think it is possible that God might just have chosen Matthew, whose gospel is written in a very orderly fashion, because he was just the kind of guy who was ideally suited to write the gospel of Matthew? Oh, I think so.

You probably know that Jesus did not teach or preach in Greek or English. It was almost certainly Aramaic, a language akin to Hebrew. One New Testament scholar, Matthew Black, has demonstrated that when some of this Sermon on the Mount is translated from Greek into Aramaic, then it comes out in poetic form. Why? Because such a form is highly memorable. Can you complete the rest of the 'poem', 'Mary had a little lamb'? If you were brought up in the UK, you would have no problem. Do you think the greatest Teacher who has ever lived might know something about how people remember things? In addition, and just in case, he also promised his Holy Spirit to help those original apostles and to guide them into all truth (Jn. 16). Do you think the all-wise God would go to all that trouble to send his Son, and not have bothered to work out how we might know about it? I think not.

You will doubtlessly have heard of *Harry Potter*. Ms Rowling, the author, before she wrote one page of the series, worked out the plot-line and end of her seventh and final book. She knew at the beginning where it will all end. Do you think God could be as smart as J. K. Rowling? Could the Almighty, omniscient God do stuff like that? Since he knows the end from the beginning, I think so. Why wouldn't he take care to prepare each of the biblical writers, including Matthew, to write down his word for our sakes? And that's why, incidentally, Matthew can draw on all these Old Testament quotations he uses, because here is the next instalment in the thrilling story of the ways of God.

Is this Sermon reliable? Of course it is. Whoever uttered these words deserves our devotion, our love and our adoration, because he is 'God with us'. If he is not that, then he deserves our utter rejection as a rampant megalomaniac who probably got what he deserved for his folly, crucifixion. The choice is as stark as that.

Is this Sermon relevant?

Let's ask this next question, since we live in a practical age. Is this Sermon relevant? People want to know, 'Does this Christianity lark work?' Skim the Sermon quickly with me. We'll just mention the Beatitudes in passing, because I am going to come back to them. The Beatitudes – everybody wants a song to sing, to find the secret of happiness, to know where they are going in this world and the next. Jesus is saying there is a way to be contented and blessed beyond your wildest dreams when God shares his life and kingdom with you. 'Blessed are the poor in spirit, for theirs is the kingdom of heaven.' When you find this dynamic relationship with God, ultimately it does not matter what is going on in your life outwardly, because you know in the end, by the grace of God, we win and inherit all things in Christ. What does the life look like for those people who are changed by the Living God to 'Beatitude type' people? Have you noticed that these Beatitudes are all plural? It's 'Blessed *are* the poor in spirit, the meek' etc. This is to be the shape of the Christian community, the characteristics that mark us out. In other words, although every individual Christian is to be undergoing transformation into the likeness of Christ, and be marked out by these qualities, none of us exhibits each of them fully.

My new two-month-old granddaughter clearly is a 'Brady' (and 'Storey'), but she has a lot of growing and developing to do before that resemblance may be recognised outside of our direct family circle. As an individual Christian, I may not have it all together, but I belong to the family of God, the community of Jesus, where these

Beatitudes and graces are not scorned and written off, but where they are nurtured, encouraged and developed. These Beatitudes are to define the shape of Christian existence and community.

What about salt and light? Is it important that the people of God should make a difference in the communities which they serve? We need the church throughout the world to be salt and light to all the putrefying communities around to make a difference, so that people then 'praise your Father in heaven'. That's not the social gospel, rather the implications of the gospel of God's grace, as 'good works' and 'good words' are joined to proclaim Jesus.

What about personal relationships? Take verses 21, 22. Here Jesus says, 'You have heard it said "Do not murder ..." But I tell you that anyone who is angry with his brother will be subject to judgement.' Why? Because murder is usually the end of a process that began in the human heart long before the fist or knife appeared. We have huge problems with domestic violence, battered wives (and sometimes husbands), abused children, date rapes and the like. See the violence that erupts any weekend in any city centre when an angry heart and a boozed brain meets opposition, whether it be another gang, the police or an individual. Does the Bible have anything to say about that? It sure does.

'You have heard that it was said, "Do not commit adultery"' (verse 27). Does the Bible have anything to say about AIDS epidemics? Does it have anything to say about human sexuality? About teenage pregnancies? Does it have anything to say about how we should behave ourselves in those intimate areas? The Bible has a lot to say. In America, more is spent on pornography than alcohol, tobacco and illicit drugs combined. Some of us blokes are looking at stuff on the Internet that would make your wife and your granny blush. And it is so addictive. Jesus has things to say about that. Is it relevant? We had better believe it.

Look what Jesus goes on to talk about off the back of immorality – the whole issue of divorce, because the two are so often related in marital breakdown. Today, the average marriage lasts about nine years: three years wedlock, three years deadlock, three years unlock – as one of my friends put it. Folk are not going the distance in marriage these days. The UK has the highest or one of the highest divorce rates in Europe and the world. And, sure enough, Jesus has things to say about that.

What about revenge? 'You have heard that it was said, "Eye for eye, and tooth for tooth." But I tell you, do not resist an evil person. If someone strikes you on the right cheek, turn to him the other also.' What does Jesus mean? Be a doormat? Well, the background of the time helps us to appreciate just what it is that he is saying. When someone intended to smack a slave, an inferior, the rule was that you used your right hand and smacked him across his right cheek with the back of your hand. To smack someone with an open, full hand was reserved for folk who were on a par with you, so you hit the left cheek. Jesus says, 'offer the other one.' So you now get a left-handed smack? No, it was taboo to use the left hand. The culture of the day forbade it. So what is Jesus saying? In effect, 'If you turn the other cheek, your assailant is going to have to smack you full in the face, and will thus be acknowledging that you are, in effect, on a par with him.' He will probably retreat embarrassed and confused.

What about generosity? Turn to chapter 6. Here we are in a world of gross injustice. Third World debt is monstrous: for every pound the Third World receives in aid, it pays three pounds in interest on debt. Hope and justice for the poor, fair trade? Jesus reminds us that generosity in the face of need, near and far, is a hallmark of his followers.

And what about prayer? What is prayer – speaking to a friendly star? Not according to Jesus. He didn't say, 'Tune into fate.' He said, 'Pray to your heavenly Father, the living, loving God.' We are witnessing a renaissance of spirituality in the western world. Much of it is far from Christian, some of it is full-on paganism. But the real alternative is the true 'New Age' teaching – Jesus has opened up a new way into the heart of the Father. Here are his master secrets on prayer: 'when you pray ...'

And forgiveness? Forgiveness is the easiest thing in the world, dead simple, until you are red raw with anger: somebody has betrayed you, hurt you and you are being asked to forgive. Have you found forgiveness easy? No, you haven't. Matthew uses a Greek word here for forgiveness, which means to let go of, send away. Imagine the pen I am now grasping tightly in my hand represents what I can't forgive. I hold it in a tight fist – I am not letting go of that thing, that person or whatever. My hand is clenched. How much then can it receive and hold? Not a lot! Forgiveness is opening your hand and letting that person/thing go. Now you are ready to receive from God.

And your money? '… where your treasure is, there your heart will be also.' I was chatting to a lady just as we left this morning's meeting. She is an older lady who has provided for her kids and grandchildren generously. But she has also left a considerable part of her estate to missions. Isn't that a wise investment? You can't take it with you but you can send it on!

While you are worrying about money, let me talk to you specifically about worry. Jesus has a whole paragraph on it. 'Do not store up for yourselves', and then verse 25, '… I tell you, do not worry'. Jesus says about your circumstances, '… I've got it all under control'. If you want something to worry about, here's what it should be: 'worry, concern yourself about my kingdom' (6:33). Live by a bigger vision than just your daily needs – that huge world, for instance, that needs the love of the Lord Jesus. As an old hymn expresses it

> Through all the changing scenes in life, in trouble and in joy,
> The praises of my God shall still my heart and tongue employ.
>
> The hosts of God encamp around the dwellings of the just.
> Deliverance he affords to all who on his succour trust.
>
> Fear him, ye saints, and you will then have nothing else to fear,
> Make you his service your delight, your wants shall be his care.

Seeking the kingdom, making his service your delight; making that your 'worry' and hanging the rest. That's living with a sense of real abandonment to God and trusting him for the rest. This is not to deny our need to make wise provision; it is saying, 'Be realistic.' Get something really major to be concerned about, a big drumbeat by which to march, and you will find lots of other things really do slot into place.

We've skimmed through a couple of chapters. Are you getting the idea? Notice what happened when Jesus finished his teaching 'as one who had authority'. The 'crowds were amazed' (7:28,29). The Greek word for 'amazed' carries the idea of being 'out of one's wits', at one level. They were taken beyond themselves, astonished. Not gob-smacked, but God-smacked. Awestruck by this marvellous Teacher. He did not teach like their teachers. His teaching came with such power because he is the Word of God Incarnate.

Is this Sermon reliable? Is it relevant? What do you think?

Is it reachable?

Can anyone simply decide just to go and live out this Sermon? Let's all live by the Sermon on the Mount, the 'golden rule', and the world will be a better place. Right? Well, some say that's precisely what should happen. The Sermon is a *straightforward possibility*. The radical theologian, Don Cupitt, says, 'The way to salvation is a decision to live one's life by an absolute standard that requires of us singleness of mind, inner integrity and disinterested love.' Have you ever met anybody like that? Don, I think you need to get out more! We only need to have a good look at our own wretched, treacherous hearts to know differently There is only one person who has ever lived this Sermon in all its fullness – Jesus!

People who say we should all simply live by the Sermon on the Mount are clearly either saying one of two things. One, they have never read it. Or two, they have never understood it. Do you think the Ten Commandments are hard – like climbing Everest ? In comparison, this Sermon is reaching for the stars!

Others go to the opposite extreme – the Sermon is a *sheer impossibility*. Albert Schweitzer, the missionary doctor, believed – for reasons we won't go into here – that the Sermon offers what he called 'interim ethics'. Apparently, according to the good doctor, Jesus was expecting the kingdom to dawn in his lifetime, like any day soon. That being the case, Jesus was calling on those of his day to be really radical. However, he got it wrong, so it really has nothing to say to us in the here and now. It was misplaced idealism.

But the truth is this. This Sermon is intended to become a *staggering reality*. At its conclusion, Jesus says, 'Therefore everyone who hears these words of mine and puts them into practice' (7:24). Again, 'everyone who hears these words of mine and does not put them into practice' (7:26). He is expecting a response, you see. Later, he says, 'Heaven and earth will pass away, but my words will never pass away' (24:35). And in his last recorded words in Matthew, he adds, lest we miss it, in the words of the Great Commission, that he is sending his disciples to baptise in the name of the Father, Son and Holy Spirit and 'teaching them to obey everything that I have commanded you' (28:20). We must not therefore 'dispensationalise' his words away.

How is this possible? Come back with me to the Beatitudes. There are eight Beatitudes. Verses 11 and 12 are an intensification, a commentary on the final one, especially to do with persecution. How do we know that? Because there is a literary device Matthew has used here called an *inclusio*. An *inclusio* is when you top and tail something. Notice how the first Beatitude starts, 'Blessed are the poor in spirit, *for theirs is the kingdom of heaven*'; and how the final one ends, 'Blessed are those who are persecuted …, *for theirs is the kingdom of heaven.*' Here is the package deal about being a Christian, about being part of God's community. It is not that some folk are poor in spirit, while others are meek, so that of the eight Beatitudes on offer, you can choose which two or three you would like. Rather, they illustrate one reality. It is this quality of life that Jesus intends to reproduce in his community, the church, and ultimately in each individual Christian. This is what heaven will look like!

Do you notice where the Beatitudes start? 'Blessed are the *poor in spirit*'. Notice that it does not say, 'Blessed are the *poor-spirited*'. There are a lot of poor-spirited people around. No, Jesus means blessed are those who know they are spiritually and morally bankrupt before God, who know their need. 'Blessed are those who mourn'; not just over the loss of loved ones or over how you screwed your life up, and are now full of vain regrets. Rather, it is people who actually realise that their sins are so serious that only the coming of the Son of God himself can help them.

'Blessed are the meek'. The weak? No, meekness is not a synonym for that. Meekness is power under control. It is being tamed by the grace of God. It is your power and independence coming under his rule and reign and putting your all and your best at his disposal. Hungering and thirsting after righteousness? Are you longing to find 'rightness with God' and for his justice to be revealed in this unjust world? What a healthy spiritual sign.

How is all this possible? Firstly, because Jesus Christ is the *Revealer*. He tells us how to live. Secondly, because Jesus Christ is the *Redeemer* who has died to make it possible: '… the Son of Man did not come to be served, but to serve, and to give his life as a ransom for many' (20:28). That is why you just can't lift this Sermon out of its overall gospel context, for its great conclusion is that Jesus goes to the cross to die for us. But how does a dead Saviour help us? Thirdly, he is also the *Renewer*, he is the Risen One. He comes to break the power of cancelled sin and set the prisoner free. He comes to make men and women new as we 'change and become like little children', and so enter the kingdom (18:3).

When I was travelling to Keswick last Saturday evening, I phoned home and had a word with my grandson. I said, 'Dan, when I get back, maybe we can go and see *Spiderman*?' His reply was curt: 'You're too late, Grandad, we've just been to see it.'

You know how Spiderman got his powers, don't you? He got bitten by a radioactive spider. And since then this guy has powers and abilities that he didn't naturally have because he has been injected with something that has changed his DNA and everything else. *Pure fiction.* But here's *fact*. Jesus Christ has come to make us rich. Jesus Christ has come to make us new. Jesus Christ has come to set us free. Jesus Christ has come that we might live through him and become like him. We have been 'bitten' by something far more powerful than a radioactive spider! We have in Christ been touched and are being changed by the power of the Living God himself. We have come before him, confessing our moral and spiritual bankruptcy, and have received what he offers – the Lord Jesus himself, the Subject of the Sermon, to live in and through us.

Disappointed with Jesus

Matthew 11:1–15

by Ian Coffey

IAN COFFEY

After 12 years as Senior Minister and Team Leader at Mutley Baptist Church in Plymouth, Ian and his wife Ruth moved to Geneva in the summer of 2004. Ian is the new Senior Pastor of Crossroads International Church there. Since his ordination in 1972, Ian has divided his time between local church leadership and working in various inter-denominational Christian agencies. He has been the leader of the Spring Harvest leadership team, and has travelled extensively as a speaker, written several books, and contributed a column to the *Western Morning News*. He and Ruth, who is a nursing sister, have four grown-up sons.

Disappointed with Jesus
Matthew 11:1–15

Introduction

Tonight we deal with a difficult topic. As we reach Matthew 11, we read about Jesus going and preaching in the towns of Galilee and then Matthew introduces a very personal, poignant note. 'Where do you go for help when you feel disappointed with Jesus?' It's the situation that faced John the Baptist.

Are you the One? (verses 2,3)

I want to look first of all at a question John the Baptist sends with his disciples, 'Are you the one who was to come, or should we expect someone else?' (verse 3). Let's just take a moment to think about the man who is asking this question. John the Baptist was a remarkable man. He came from a rich spiritual heritage. His mum and his dad, Zechariah and Elizabeth, came from priestly families. In the gospel accounts, apart from the Lord Jesus, no one else has such detail recorded about the circumstances of his birth. He was a child of promise, of prophecy and prayer. If you turn with me to Luke 1, you will see something of what Luke records as the message to John the Baptist's parents in Luke 1 verse 13

… the angel said to him: 'Do not be afraid, Zechariah; your prayer has been heard. Your wife Elizabeth will bear you a son, and you are to give him the name John. He will be a joy and delight to you, and many will rejoice because of his birth, for he will be great in the sight of the Lord. He is never to take wine or other fermented drink, and he will be filled with the Holy Spirit even from birth. Many of the people of Israel will he bring back to the Lord their God. And he will go on before the Lord, in the spirit and power of Elijah, to turn the hearts of the fathers to their children and the disobedient to the wisdom of the righteous – to make ready a people prepared for the Lord' (Lk. 1:13–17).

John the Baptist was a significant man; the circumstances of his birth trumpeted something of that significant life. We remember John's remit was very clear. He had three things to do – to clear the way for the Lord, to prepare the way of the Lord and then to get out of the way of the Lord. His simple text was 'Repent, the kingdom of God is arriving' and as he preached that message of repentance and that was demonstrated in people acknowledging their need of God's forgiveness by being baptised, he spoke of One who would come after him. 'I baptise with water,' says John, 'but One comes after me whose sandals I am not worthy to unloose and he will baptise you with the Holy Spirit.' And when his disciples came to him and said, 'Lots of people are going after Jesus', John's comment was, 'He must increase and I must decrease.' Here was a man who understood his ministry. Clear the way for the Lord, prepare the way for the Lord and then get out of the way of the Lord.

Jesus and John the Baptist were cousins and I wonder at what point God revealed to John that Jesus was the Messiah? It was his great privilege to point to Jesus: 'Behold, the Lamb of God who bears away the sin of the world.' The One who has come to end the whole sacrificial system, God's perfect sacrifice, Jesus the long-awaited Messiah. John was a remarkable man with a special mission but where is he in Matthew 11:2?

He is in prison. How did he get there? He got there because as a man of righteousness he spoke about the need for people to get right with God. Herod, who was on the throne at the time, had taken his half-brother Philip's wife Herodias to be his own wife. John the Baptist was fearless. When he talked about sin, he talked not only about the sin of ordinary people but even pointed to the royal throne and he said what Herod had done was wrong – it was not pleasing to God. John was taken and thrown into prison and he would never see freedom from that prison cell. He would know the ultimate freedom of being released into the presence of God but he would die the death of execution.

Have I made a mistake?

What's going on? Why, at this particular point, in Matthew's gospel, does Matthew break off from his great detailed account of the ministry of Jesus? Suddenly a message comes. John, the one who had prepared the way of the Lord, who had been so faithful is asking a deep question: 'Are you the one who is to come, or have I made a terrible mistake?' Turn back to Matthew 3:11,12

> I baptise you with water for repentance. But after me will come one who is more powerful than I, whose sandals I am not fit to carry. He will baptise you with the Holy Spirit and with fire. His winnowing fork is in his hand, and he will clear his threshing-floor, gathering his wheat into the barn and burning up the chaff with unquenchable fire.

This was the message that John had brought; that there was going to come judgement. Yet what he was hearing about was Jesus healing, and seeing people oppressed by demonic spirits being released. What John had expected was not being fulfilled and there was the prophet of the wilderness, who lived a rather nomadic, ascetic lifestyle, suddenly confined to a very small prison, no longer ministering to crowds, feeling the pain and ache of loneliness, perhaps even wondering why Jesus hadn't visited him there. He was beginning to feel doubts: 'I wonder if I made a dreadful mistake.' Even this great powerful servant of God found doubt gnawed away at his heart.

A number of years ago I was invited to share a seminar with Elisabeth Elliot, the widow of Jim Elliot of Auca fame – the author of *Shadow of the Almighty*. I was asked to share a seminar with her on the subject of suffering. We had a telephone call and she said, 'What are we going to do?' I said, 'I'll tell you exactly what we are going to do. I'll carry your Bible, I'm going to change your overhead projector slides, I'm going to pour your water and I'm going to pray for you as you tell us about suffering. I have nothing to say.' She was a very gracious lady and we did actually do the seminar together and we learned a great deal but I remember as we sat and began to prepare that seminar, she said, 'Here's my definition – suffering is having what you don't want and wanting what you don't have.' John the Baptist was there – he had what he didn't want, he was in prison. And he was wanting what he didn't have, assurance that Jesus was fulfilling the programme that John had announced that he would fulfil. 'Are you the one who was to come, or should we look for another?'

I don't know what you are afraid of. I don't like heights particularly, I made it once to the top of the Eiffel Tower and stood with my back to the wall, clinging anxiously, as the family said, 'Look Dad, look Dad!' 'OK, it's a wonderful view,' I said, with my eyes tightly screwed up. Some years ago a job needed doing on the roof of the house and the house had a very, very high roof. I got the ladder out and I climbed up and I managed to get onto the roof and fix what needed to be fixed but then came the moment of having to get off the roof and onto the ladder and I had to swing my leg out into outer space, it felt like, before I could get it onto the rung of the ladder. I couldn't do it. I could not do it. I'd been gone for quite some time and Ruth thought, 'he's unusually quiet,' and she came out and had a look and said, 'I could tell immediately by the colour of you that you weren't feeling very well.' So she came upstairs and stuck her head out of the bathroom window. She said, 'Look, I'll do anything I can, I'll hold the ladder, I'll tie it to the railings.'

We named it, we claimed it, we did everything, she played Graham Kendrick's choruses loudly over the tannoy but I could not move. I was absolutely frozen and paralysed with fear. In the end she said, 'This is ridiculous, it's getting dark, there's nothing for it, I'm going to have to go and phone the fire brigade.' That was my defining moment. We lived in a little village and I thought, I have a choice. I can die of embarrassment or I can die of a broken neck. I could not live in that village with the knowledge that I had had to get the fire brigade to get me off the roof and by faith, I swung my leg over the side of the gutter and I am here to this day. I now pay people to go up ladders onto roofs. But here is the lesson I learned, it's possible to be paralysed, it's possible to lose perspective, it's possible not just to be frozen on a roof but frozen in your faith because you are disappointed with Jesus. Jesus has not acted in the way that we would expect and there is that gnawing doubt within. All of the singing, all of the fellowship, all of the rich teaching – some of us, if we are honest, would say, 'I am disappointed Lord.'

What is Jesus doing?

John, in prison, asks a question. What does Jesus do (verses 4–6)? Jesus says, 'I want you to go back and tell John what you hear and what you see.' There is a lovely little statement about the Lord Jesus that comes in Matthew 12. It's from the prophet, Isaiah 42. Matthew has this habit in his gospel of saying, 'Oh, this is to fulfil the Old Testament Scripture that says ...' and he does it there in 12:18

> Here is my servant whom I have chosen, the one I love, in whom I delight; I will put my Spirit on him, and he will proclaim justice to the nations. He will not quarrel or cry out; no-one will hear his voice in the streets. A bruised reed he will not break, and a smouldering wick he will not snuff out ...

The first prayer my mother ever taught me to pray was 'Gentle Jesus, meek and mild.' Often we have said that it's an unhelpful image because somehow or another it portrays a weak view of Christ and we want to say he is strong, he is the King of Kings, he is the Lord of Lords, but he is the gentle Jesus. The smouldering wick is safe in his hands, the smouldering wick he doesn't put out and the bruised reed he doesn't break. And Jesus doesn't send John a rebuke. He doesn't say, 'Keep the faith.' He does three things. He sends back the message: 'Look at what God is doing, look at the story of those who are seeing again, those who are walking, the deaf hearing, the dead raised, good news being preached to the poor. Tell John in that prison cell, whose vision has become limited, tell him what God is doing.'

We need to have our eyes opened. Our problem is, so often, we look at our church, we look at our family and we interpret what is not happening there as what is not happening in the wider world, in the kingdom of God. John had lost perspective 'Tell him what you see.' Jesus too is sending a code – remember what God has said. John knew the book of Isaiah, he knew it well. He knew it because it spoke of his own role and his ministry. He thought about it often as he prepared to be the one who prepared the way of the Lord and the Lord Jesus, by sending that particular message back to him, is reminding him of those Scriptures. Take Isaiah 35:5,6, this is what it said about the coming of God's servant: 'Then will the eyes of the blind be opened and the ears of the deaf unstopped. Then will the lame leap like a deer, and the mute tongue shout for joy.' John, remember what's written down, remember what the book says, remember what God promised. And then again in Isaiah 61:1: 'The Spirit of the Sovereign LORD is on me', says the Lord's servant, 'because the LORD has anointed me to bring good news to the poor.' John, remember the next bit: 'He has sent me to bind up the broken-hearted, to proclaim freedom for the captives and release from darkness for the prisoners, to proclaim the year of the LORD's favour and the day of vengeance of our God'. The coded message, as he points him back to what God has written, is simply this – this is God's agenda, God's timetable.

Blessed is the man …

Then he adds that wonderful little statement in verse 6. 'Blessed is the man who does not fall away on account of me.' Literally, blessed is the one who doesn't stumble on account of me, doesn't trip up because of me. In gentleness and tenderness he says, 'Look at what God is doing.' Remember what God has said and trust God to work it out. I have a strong conviction on my heart that that is a word for many of us here. 'Blessed is the one who does not stumble on account of me.' We can't understand what the Lord is doing, we prayed about that child, that member of the family and those prayers have yet to be answered. Nothing seems to be breaking through and it's been a relief this week to come to Keswick, yet you know the reality is that Monday morning, you face that situation again. Listen to the words of Jesus: 'Blessed is the one who does not fall away, doesn't stumble, on account of me.'

Many of us, I guess, have reason to thank God for the ministry of David Watson. I would say that he helped me greatly through his books, through his preaching, through his teaching. I remember going to a conference a matter of months before David was called home. He couldn't speak, he was due to speak at the conference and he couldn't attend but he sent a tape and it was a very surreal experience to sit in a room with 400 other leaders and to hear David's voice, having been recorded a couple of days before, struggling for breath, coming over the loud-speaker system. I have never forgotten what he said. He said, 'You know, these weeks I haven't been able to do a great deal but they have been really special as God has ministered to me by his Spirit. One of the most wonderful things that I have discovered in the last few weeks as I have just been able to read my Bible, pray, listen to others read the Scriptures is this: God has shown me, if I am never to preach another sermon, never to write another word, never to attend another conference, he couldn't love me any more or less than he loves me now.' Do you rejoice in knowing him, having that knowledge of sins forgiven and the hope of heaven, that inexpressible joy full of glory that even comes in those dark, dark moments?

Jesus endorses John (verses 7–15)

Notice verses 7–15, this remarkable declaration that the Lord Jesus gives about John the Baptist. As John's disciples were leaving, Jesus began to speak to the crowd about John. I often get asked to write references for people and I'll confess to you there are times when I don't know quite what to say. I read of a reference recently where somebody wrote 'Anyone who can get this man to work for them will be most fortunate' – you can read that either way. When we were clearing out the house some time ago Ruth came across one of my school reports, much to my discomfort, and she took great delight in sharing the contents. One teacher wrote on the little comment column on my report card: 'If Ian spent as much time doing work as he does avoiding it, he would be a genius.'

What does the Lord Jesus say, what's the reference he gives?

> What did you go out into the desert to see? A reed swayed by the wind? If not, what did you go out to see? A man dressed in fine clothes? No, those who wear fine clothes are in kings' palaces. Then what did you go out to see? A prophet? Yes, I tell you and more than a prophet.

Jesus praises John's strength. He praises his sense of purpose. He praises his diligence, his faithfulness to the task. What an endorsement from the lips of Jesus. You know John Brown, the great champion of the cause of the slaves? At his funeral, Wendell Phillips, in his oration acknowledging John Brown, said this: 'How some men struggle into obscurity while others forget themselves into immortality.' Forget themselves into immortality. Jesus acknowledges that great servant.

Some of you looked at the verse and puzzled and you are right, it is a puzzling verse. Verse 11, 'I tell you the truth: Among those born of women there has not risen anyone greater than John the Baptist; yet he who is least in the kingdom of heaven is greater than he.' What does it mean? John came as the last of the great Old Testament prophets; he was the Elijah that the Jews believed would return before the Lord would come. That's what Jesus says (verse 14), 'if you [can] accept it, he is the Elijah', he comes in the spirit of Elijah. 'He who has ears, let him hear', says Jesus. But the greatness of John the Baptist and all that came before the cross and the resurrection fades in comparison to the high position that the youngest believer has since the great Easter event and the gift of the Spirit. John marked the end of an era and the beginning of another one. What Jesus is saying is in the kingdom of heaven there is room. He was a great man, no one born among woman greater than he, says Jesus, and yet the least, the smallest Christian with the weakest faith this side of the cross occupies a special place in the kingdom of heaven. Thank God for that privilege. And I felt as I studied these words something of that echo of what we read in Scripture, of the Lord Jesus welcoming his children into heaven with that 'Well done, good and faithful servant.' There are some of us who carry heavy loads, who have known what it is to suffer. Folk who are faithful under fire. We are reminded of the declaration that Jesus made about John that all who work well will receive that 'Well done, good and faithful servant.'

You know that old Aesop's fable about the hare and the tortoise? Remember the hare sets off at a great pace and seems to be winning the race and then falls asleep and the tortoise plods on through and gets there in the end? We live in a generation when the hare seems to be praised all the time and what we desperately need are tortoises. Remember what William Carey said, 'I can plod.' What a great testimony. 'I can hang in there, I don't look for the quick fix, the quick blessing, the instant solution but I can plod.' God says to some of you here this evening, 'Well done, good and faithful servant.'

A concert pianist, at the end of a recital, was being applauded by the audience warmly and the call for an encore came. The pianist went to the side of the stage and the stage manager said, 'They are calling for an encore' and the pianist said, 'No, I'm not going to play one tonight.' 'Come on, they are calling for you; look, they're standing.' He said, 'No, they are not all standing.' 'Of course they are. Look, you can see.' 'No,' the pianist said. 'If you look up in the balcony, third row from the left, there is a man with an overcoat and he's not standing.' The stage manager said, 'What does he know?' He said, 'Well, he's been teaching me to play the piano since I was five. If he was standing and everyone else was sat down then I'd go out and play an encore.'

Bring your disappointment to him

Eyes are watching you and watching me. Who is it that we seek to impress? Jesus reminds us of that 'Well done, good and faithful servant' and then, jumping to the end of the chapter and the in-between part, you can read about Jesus using this opportunity to talk about his generation being like children and speaking strong words of judgement to Korazin and Bethsaida because of their hardness of heart and their blindness to what the miracles signified. And then verse 25, Jesus praises God. He praises his Father for the way that truth has been revealed to those who trust and follow, particularly verse 28, 'Come to me, all you who are weary and burdened, and I will give you rest. Take my yoke upon me and learn from me, for I am gentle and humble in heart, and you will find rest for your souls. For my yoke is easy and my burden is light.' This is an invitation. We have read of a question, an answer, a declaration – here is the invitation and it's an invitation to you and to me. I do not know what you have been carrying in your life in these past months or maybe years but I wonder if John the Baptist's story brings hope to your heart. For some of us, it may be an issue to do with family, a breakdown in health, the disappointment of Christians who we thought so much of who have let us down, the pain of a church split, the onset of illness and infirmity that's put us in the place where we are no longer able to be at the centre but having to stand or sit on the sidelines. Jesus knows. Jesus cares. We can trust in him. Bring that disappointment to him. Bring that sense of need to him and discover his ability to strengthen us.

Ask, seek and knock

Turn to one last chapter, Matthew 7. You know that famous passage 'Ask and it will be given to you; seek and you will find; knock and the door will be opened to you' there in Matthew 7:7. Wonderful illustration Jesus gives about a son and his dad. Four weeks ago I had the thrill of conducting the wedding of my eldest son, Chris, the second of my sons to get married. Just before the service, we were in a church, not my own church, another church along the south coast, and that particular church had to bring in a registrar from outside, so minutes to go before the bride was arriving, we were checking with the registrar that the details were correct and I was cleared to take the service. We got to the end of it all and then the registrar looked at Chris and said, 'That will be £43.50, please.' And he said 'Pardon?' She said, '£43.50. You remember we discussed the attendance fee and the certificate.' Then he looked at me and said, 'Dad, I haven't got any money.' And the registrar said, 'If you were just the minister and not his dad, what would you do?' I said, 'Let's not go into that right now.' I rustled around and I managed to come up with about 25 quid, I stuck my head round the door and Ruth was sat in the church. I called her out and said, 'Have you got any money?' 'Why are you asking me that?' 'Just give me what you've got.' Between the two of us, we managed to eke out £43.50. I honestly thought I was going to have to go in and stop the service and say, 'We need to have a love offering.' Don't you just love kids?

Three days later as I drove along, smiling at the memory, the Lord Jesus reminded me of these words: 'Which of you, if his son asks for bread, will give him a stone? Or if he asks for a fish, will give him a snake?' Or, if he says, 'Dad, I need £43.50', will say, 'On your bike son?' 'If you, then, [who] are evil, know how to give good gifts to your children, how much more [how much more, how much more] will your Father in heaven give good gifts to those [of his children grown up enough to ask for them.]'

Friends, when was the last time, with honesty, you said 'Dad, I haven't got any money?'

Christian Ministry – the Cost and the Celebration

Matthew 14:32–21

by Keith White

KEITH WHITE

Keith was born, bred and converted near Liverpool and following a Business Studies degree and work experience went on to become a curate in Edinburgh and then Sheffield. He was Rector of Holy Trinity Norwich from 1987–1995 before working for the Evangelical Fellowship of Zimbabwe with Crosslinks Mission Society for two years. As well as serving as a Keswick Trustee he is a director of Christian Youth Ministries and Inspire Christian Counselling and is currently Vicar at St John's Church, Ipswich. He is married to Gaynor with three children and remains a steadfast Everton supporter!

Christian Ministry – the Cost and the Celebration

Matthew 14:13–21

Introduction

Let me start with a penetrating question. How are you doing? Quite a lot of people have asked me this week. 'How are you, Keith?' To which I universally answer, 'I'm fine, things are going great.' Yet, if the truth were known, it's been a difficult year. Lots of hard work, lots of pressure. We've got three children and they make their demands. There don't seem to be enough hours in the day to accomplish all that we would like to do. By the grace of God, the church back in Ipswich has been growing and that's wonderful. But it's not been easy.

Many of us have come to Keswick with heavy hearts, one way or another. Some of us are exhausted. Some of us are tired of having to be the strong ones in our local fellowship, our home group, our family. Some of us have been giving and giving and giving in all sorts of ways and we are quite worn out.

And often we go back from events like this, into the same situations, pretty much the same people. Maybe we don't allow God to address us in events like this.

You've heard of the family on their way to church. They've had an argument the night before, the mother and the father aren't speaking to each other, the children had to be dragged out of bed and thrown into the back of the car. An air of broody silence covers the whole family. They get out of the car in the church car park, go in through the outer doors of the church building, through the decompression chamber. In through the inner doors of the church building and suddenly everything's fantastic. 'How are you doing?' 'We're fine. Praise the Lord.' And then we go out again, completely untouched by the whole experience.

What interests me about Jesus is the way that so often, he'd say 'Enough is enough for now, we're heading off. Come and get in a boat. We're going for a little sail. I'm going to escape from this just for a little while.'

In fact Jesus often would be getting into a boat. In all the gospels, there are boats involved. Jesus called the fisherman from their boats. In Matthew 8, the storm at sea, Jesus is asleep in a boat. Chapter 9:1, they take a boat trip because they need a break. Chapter 13, the parables; where were they spoken from? From a boat, that was his pulpit. It was a place of relaxation, a place for journeying and for teaching and preaching from.

In 1986 they dug up one of these first century Palestinian Galilean fishing boats, 28 foot long. If Jesus were among us today, it would probably be a people carrier. And 'Let's just have a couple of hours off, guys. Let's get in the people carrier and we're off.' It could be used to travel from place to place. He could call mechanics to follow him, 'Leave your garage and follow me. You've been involved in fixing engines but, from now on, I'm going to make you fixers of men'.

Imagine Jesus and his disciples in the people carrier travelling from place to place. James and John in the back, arguing. The mother of James and John coming to Jesus and saying, 'Could my sons sit one on either side of you when you come in your people carrier?' Peter, if they ever let him drive the thing, would be done for speeding. Thomas would be forever stopping and checking the tyre pressure ...

There were times when Jesus needed to escape the crowds and Jesus would find himself in a remote spot and the crowds would follow him. Matthew 14:13: 'When Jesus heard what had happened, he withdrew by boat privately to a solitary place.' And there follows, as the crowd follows him, the feeding of the 5,000, a story that is so familiar to us. One of the reasons it is so familiar to us is it's the only miracle, apart from the resurrection, that appears in all four gospels. We are very familiar with the incident which teaches us so much about Jesus and about the ministry that God calls us to.

Let's go back to the question, 'How are you doing?' For many of us, it's been hard work, it's been tough in our local churches. We've been giving and giving. We're having to stand up for truth, maybe we're a minister, an elder, a home group leader, a Sunday group leader, a children's leader, a youth leader, maybe we're involved in all kinds of caring roles in the church. Frankly we're worn out, disillusioned, disappointed. I think this story, very familiar though it may be, is instructive for us.

The cost of Christian ministry

When I talk about Christian ministry I'm talking about every Christian. We are all called as Christians to exercise a ministry. So the cost of exercising that ministry over this past year in our local churches – what's it been like?

There was a cost for Jesus. Verse 13, begins, 'When Jesus heard what had happened ...' What had happened? John the Baptist is beheaded. John, who courageously stood up to Herod's immoral ways, pays for that courage with his life. Jesus must have been distressed. Lazarus, when he died, Jesus wept at his graveside. I'm sure Jesus felt this deeply. John the Baptist prepared the way for the coming of Christ: now his role is over. Jesus is left centre stage, it is his ministry. When he heard these things, 'he withdrew by boat privately to a solitary place'. He needed space; time to refocus, time in prayer.

If you glance on to Mark chapter 1:21–39, take a look at a day in the life of Jesus. See the need for him to both minister and get away.

Teaching, casting out demons; it's tiring, giving of yourself in that way. A great opportunity to have the preacher home for lunch, verse 29, maybe a chance for putting your feet up for an hour or two?

'Simon's mother-in-law was in bed with a fever and they told Jesus about her. So he went to her, took her hand and helped her up. The fever left …', so there's a healing ministry now. Maybe there's an opportunity in the evening to relax because preachers get time off, even on Sundays. Verse 32, 'That evening after sunset the people brought to Jesus all the sick and demon-possessed. The whole town gathered at the door, and Jesus healed many who had various diseases.' That's what I call a busy day.

But he's a preacher so it's only one day a week, surely. 'Six days invisible, one day incomprehensible', that's what they say. Maybe a chance for a long lie-in the next morning? Alas, in verse 35 we're told that 'Very early in the morning, while it was still dark, Jesus got up, left the house and went to a solitary place where he prayed.' He needed to do that. He needed space. He needed time. And we do too.

We're too busy by half, aren't we? We organise schedules for ourselves that guarantee we don't know that intimacy with God. I know I'm a vicar so I don't really understand about real work. I was at the hairdresser a while ago, hadn't been there before, and the chappie who was cutting, said to me, 'What do you do?' Things always go wrong when I say I'm a vicar and it's either this awkward silence, not only between me and him but also the rest of the place, or he asks some deep theological question that I've never thought of before and haven't a clue how to answer. Have you ever had those moments where you're talking to somebody and at the end of conversation, the only thing you are sure of is that you shouldn't have started it in the first place? I thought maybe I would try a different tack this time and not say I'm a vicar, so I said to him, 'I teach the Christian faith.' There was a long pause and then he said, 'Is that a full-time job?'

We are all so busy. Some of us have got young families and life just gets busier and busier. Some of us are involved in the business world and we are doing more and more with less and less time. We've got less and less people to do it and more and more work. I came across one chap who told me: 'Something sick is happening at our workplace. It is so demanding, so ruthless, that I used to leave my hat on the door on the way into the office, now I leave my heart. And the worrying thing is, when it's time to return home, I often forget to pick it up again. I don't have the time or emotional energy for anything any more.' There comes a time when we've got to withdraw, have time with God, time to recharge.

It doesn't get any better, I gather, at retirement. 'Retirement's all well and good,' I heard one chap say, 'but it's really a job for the younger boys.'

I don't want to shrink wrap all the things that matter most to me in my life. When people go through a crisis, a near-death experience or something like that, they always say: 'It's reorientated my life. I now know that people matter most to me. It's my relationships, my relationship with God, my marriage, my children, my colleagues, my neighbours.' Why wait for the crisis before discovering that?

There is a cost in Christian ministry. There is a price to be paid. Some of us have paid it over this past year. And we are suffering for it. Some of us look back on our Christian lives and there was a time when there was much joy and enthusiasm, early days when we gave ourselves wholeheartedly to God and to other people and we were all geared up and we were vessels of God's love to needy people. We give and give and give. And one day we discover a tinge of resentment in the ministry that we're exercising in our church. We bury the warning signal and give more and more and more, even though our heart may not be in it in quite the same way. We press on until, finally, it was just a little thing, suddenly the roof caves in and 'This is nuts' we say. 'Who cares for me? I'm empty on the inside. I'm angry, I'm hurt, I'm confused. I'm running on empty.'

On a regular basis, Jesus would say, 'Enough is enough for now.' He gave enormous amounts of himself. Up a mountain he would go to pray, rest, recuperate and refocus. Go on a boat with a few friends.

And when we get exhausted we often get way out of perspective the things that happen to us. I spoke to a lady just a week or two ago. She said to me, 'There is no love in the fellowship to which I belong.' I have to say it was more a comment about her than it was about the fellowship. She was exhausted. Everything had got out of perspective. There is a cost involved and some of us have had a tough time of it.

The compassion involved in Christian ministry

Verse 13b, 'Hearing of this, the crowds followed him on foot from the towns. When Jesus landed and saw a large crowd, he had compassion on them'. He healed their sick.

It's bound to happen to Jesus. He creates the space, he has a time to withdraw and be on his own, time with his disciples. He creates the space but, verse 14, the place is packed out with people who followed him. Back in chapter 9 verse 36, he saw the crowds harassed and helpless, sheep without a shepherd, aimlessly drifting in an uncertain world; he had compassion on them. The feeding of the 4,000 in the next chapter, he has compassion on them. The blind men are healed in chapter 20 of Matthew's gospel. Why? Because Jesus had compassion on them.

There was time for himself, but he was never one of those people who modelled this, 'Finger on my own pulse all the time, always worried about me, making sure I'm looked after.' He knew the importance of getting away but he knew the value of people. He had compassion. It's the same word that appears in the parable of the Good Samaritan. The Good Samaritan was compassionate to the man who had been beaten up. I've heard a lot of sermons on the Good Samaritan, I've read a lot about it and I've never once heard a positive comment about the priest and the Levite who walked by on the other side. But I've got a bit of sympathy for them. They are probably on their way to a meeting. The priest and the Levite were probably thinking to themselves, as they passed by this man, 'It's all right for you, at least the day's over as far as you're concerned. We've got four more meetings to handle.'

I know we need space but we can become so precious about ourselves. As we pray for the Father's heart, we pray for a heart of compassion that reaches out to people in need. Jesus was always doing that, always thinking about people, putting their needs before his own. And a single act of compassion can turn somebody's life. Even a look, a word, can go a long, long way.

Jesus was always thinking about people. From Day One of their apprenticeship training, Jesus sought to establish the priority of people in the minds of his disciples. It wasn't always easy. Remember how the disciples would always put something else in front of other people, be it their schedules or popularity or power or money or comforts or convenience? Patiently but firmly, Jesus would rearrange their values and say, 'It's about loving and restoring people, serving and empowering people.' Jesus modelled that compassion into the lives of others throughout his ministry, even on the most difficult day of his life. On a cross, what was he doing? Thinking of his mother. 'John, would you look after her?' Just before his last breath, thinking of that dying thief, one more lost person to save.

There's a lot of talk these days about compassion fatigue. We see the pictures on the television and our senses are dulled to the need around us. But compassion fatigue can extend to our ministries within the church, can't it? We've been giving and giving and we've become a little cynical because we are run down on the inside. There is a cost involved in Christian ministry which should lead us to seek out those places and times of solitude, to withdraw and to be quiet. And there is compassion involved in Christian ministry. It is people that we are serving.

The challenge of Christian ministry

The crowd stay and Jesus ministers to them. They are in a remote place and it's getting late and the disciples are very concerned about the food supply; you know the story. Let's focus on verse 16. 'You give them something to eat', he says. You can imagine the stunned silence that followed that instruction. John records in his gospel that Philip says immediately after this, 'Eight months' wages are not enough for everyone here just to have a little bite to eat.' It is amazing; when you ask something sacrificial, some men become experts at mental arithmetic. Peter, ever helpful says, 'Well, got a boy's picnic lunch. Five little loaves and a couple of sardines. That should feed, let's see... that should feed, em, just the boy really.' Don't suppose his mother, when she was packing the lunch in the morning, thought, 'Just a bit extra... maybe there's going to be 5,000 families.' We're not meant to miss the hopelessness of the whole situation. John reminds us in his gospel that Jesus was testing his disciples because he knew what he was going to do and he certainly didn't expect the disciples to produce food from nowhere. He was hoping that they would express their trust in him. Faith is like a muscle that grows with exercise, becomes stronger through being tested and challenged.

Here's the challenge. Jesus says to them, 'You give them something to eat.' They didn't rise to the challenge. Nor did they learn from the challenge because, chapter 15:33, his disciples said to him, this is after the feeding of the 5,000: 'Where could we [find] enough bread in this remote place to feed such a crowd?' It's amazing how many times God answers our prayers and we still don't learn.

I can imagine Matthew writing this gospel, having the time of his life at this point. Matthew 16:5, 'When they went across the lake, the disciples forgot to take [the] bread.' Jesus has to respond to them, chapter 16:8, 'Aware of their discussion, Jesus asked, "You of little faith, why are you talking among yourselves about having no bread? Do you still not understand? Don't you remember the five loaves for the five thousand, and how many basketfuls you gathered?"' The Bread of Life offers himself as the answer to the spiritually hungry. 'Place your faith in me, trust me in this', is what he is saying.

Back to chapter 14:16, Jesus says to them, 'You give them something to eat.' There is a needy world all around us, searching for spiritual food, hungry for life and significance. I guess that we make one of two opposite mistakes in response to the invitation to give a hungry world spiritual food. Our response falls into two wrong categories. One is, 'We'll do it' and the other is, 'We won't do it'. They both seem equally wrong to me.

'We can do it,' say some. 'We have the resources, the money, the talents, the experience. We can feed the crowd, no problem. We can preach the gospel to the ends of the earth and make disciples of all nations, no problem. We have the technology. Our minister's a brilliant minister. He can do anything. You should see our services, they're wonderful.' There was a church like that in Revelation 3 in Sardis. The notice sheet there looks like a railway timetable. The place is packed out. There is so much energy in the worship, there is so much power in the preaching. It's alive. But according to Jesus himself, it wasn't. 'You have a reputation for being alive,' he said, 'but actually you're dead.' It's a reputation but no matching inward reality. We are trying to do things on our own. Who needs Jesus? We'll manage fine in our local church, we don't need the prayer meeting. We're not dependent on anybody for anything. Take a reality check. How can we possibly feed people from our own resources? We'll impress them maybe, even interest them. But nothing of eternal significance will be achieved.

Some say, 'We can't do it. Look at the people here, thousands of them. We've just got a picnic lunch to work from. It's impossible. The job's too big, we don't have the resources, our minister's rubbish. We're not like one of those big churches that have loads of people and a committee for everything and money dribbling out of every-body's ears. We've taken a spiritual inventory of our place and what we've come up with is five little bits of bread and a couple of fishes and that's your lot. Give them something to eat. You must be joking. We can't.' So people are scavenging for spiritual reality and feeding off empty substitutes while we deprive them of the Bread of Life.

So verse 15, the response is 'Send them away, we can't cope.' Yet the miracle of this story is meagre resources in the hands of Jesus go a lot further than we can ever dare imagine.

'I can't do very much.' 'You've got a great gift.' 'Oh, it's not much.' 'I don't think that I have a very important role to play.' I don't suppose the boy thought he had a great role to play when he brought his lunch for a picnic that day; see what Jesus did with that which was offered to him.

Remember Mary took that jar of perfume and she broke it over Jesus as an anointing for him before his burial. The disciples were all grumbling and said, 'We could have sold that.' Everybody takes an interest in selling things and giving to the poor when they see it used in another way in terms of worship and sacrifice. They're all criticising and Jesus says, 'Leave her alone. She's done a beautiful thing to me. She did what she could.' Isn't that liberating? Do what you can. That's all God asks from us. He's given us certain gifts, he wants us to use them. You say, 'Oh, it's not much.' Give it to him. Don't say, 'Send the people away.' It's not what we do and it's not what we don't do, it's we bring it to Jesus.

When I was a lad, I used to ask my father if he could give me some money so I could buy him a birthday present. And my father never expected more from me than he gave me in the first place. God is the same. He doesn't expect more from us than he's given us in the first place. Do what you can. Give what you can.

Mary did what she could but she did everything she could because that jar of perfume represented something very precious. It was worth a year's wages. It represented the wholeheartedness of her devotion. 'Here it is, I give it to you. It's yours, Lord Jesus. Use it as you will, it's yours. I'm available.'

If I'd been there, I like to think I would have got that jar of perfume because I'm a follower of Christ and I know what I would have done. I would have got the jar of expensive perfume, brought it to Jesus, whipped out one of those little measuring spoons, poured a little bit and poured it on Jesus, 'There's your worship, Jesus. I'm being a careful steward. Nothing sacrificial, nothing over the top. Just want to give you my worship. There's it back.'

Mary broke the whole jar and poured it over Jesus as a mark of her worship. Jesus said 'She's done something for me that stretches far further than she could possibly imagine. What's she done will be told as a memorial for her.' I don't suppose she thought all that through when she went to get the jar of perfume. Do what you can, but do everything you can. Give it the very best that you've got.

Verse 18, Jesus says, 'Bring them here to me, the bread and the fishes. Bring those resources and the people who are hungry. Don't send them away. Bring them to me.' 'Send them away' and 'bring them to me.' That's the church's and Christ's offer, it seems sometimes. They're saying, 'We can't cope' and Jesus said, 'Bring them to me.' It's not 'We can do it' or 'We can't do it'. It's 'Bring them to me.' Bring them in your prayers and bring them as you invite them and bring them as you encourage them towards faith. 'Bring them to me, I can do amazing things with your lack of resources. Just bring them to me.'

In John 1, Andrew follows Jesus and goes to bring Simon Peter to Jesus. The text in John 1 says, 'he brought him to Jesus.' Archbishop William Temple, in his commentary on John's gospel, simply says 'It's the greatest thing one person can do for another.' So the challenge for us is – whatever we have, whatever our role is, whatever part we play, 'bring it to me. Don't send the people away.' 'I will use you to feed them,' he says.

The co-operation in Christian ministry

Notice the way that Jesus involves his disciples at every step through this miracle. The people sit down; the other gospel writers tell us that the disciples organised the seating plan. He thanks God, breaks the bread, gives it to the disciples, the disciples give it to the people, the disciples gather it up again. There's 12 basketfuls left over, one each for the disciples, I guess. They've all got their own participation in this miracle, they've been involved, they've seen the results, they themselves are fulfilled. They've got blessings over and more besides. Jesus could have done the manna in the wilderness thing where there was a self-service arrangement but he used the disciples to share in this miraculous event. He sought their co-operation. And they all ate and were satisfied and the leftovers were the over-whelming provision of God. It's about teamwork, partnership. It's Christ with us. And us, as the church together, bringing our meagre resources to him and bringing them together to him.

I heard a story recently, told by Jim Roberts that's quoted in the Willowcreek material. Jim Roberts visited a class of schoolchildren and was there observing the teacher playing a game with the children. The game was called 'Balloon Stomp'. All the children had to have a balloon tied to their ankle and all the children had to go around stomping on each other's balloons while protecting their own. Whenever their balloon was popped, the child had to go to the side and sit down until at the end of the game there was one person with their balloon intact and they were the winner. And it was a ruthless game. It was not a community-building event.

Eventually one child had the balloon intact at the end and they were the winner.

Then Roberts said something disturbing happened. Another class came in to play the same game but this time the class were a special needs class. People with a mental handicap. Roberts said he started to get a sick feeling in his stomach. The whistle blew and the children didn't have much clue as to what was going on because the explanation had been brief. They got the idea of bursting balloons so they played the game but not exactly in the same way as the previous group. Instead of protecting their own balloon, instead of chasing everyone else around, they began intentionally to help each other, getting their balloons stomped on. So one little girl would kneel down, hold her balloon on the ground and another boy came along and stamped on it. And she congratulated him for it and then popped his balloon and he thanked her for it. And all over the room, children were helping each other until every balloon was popped and then as the last one popped all the children applauded and cheered because all the balloons were popped and together they had got the job done and no one was left out and nobody lost and everybody won.

The question is, which class got the game right and which got it wrong and which game are we going to play when it comes to our church life? Because there's only one of two ways of going through life. One is, we live in community and we'll team together and we co-operate and we work together. The other is, we're on our own, we're a lone Christian.

God calls people to the missionfield. Keswick's known for it. But wouldn't it be great to have people standing up tonight to say, 'I'm staying where I am. I'm going to be more committed to my local church. I've been drifting. I've been disappointed. I'm hurting. I'm weary. But I want to stand, to receive the Father's heart of compassion, to bring what meagre resources I have to God and say "I'm available in my local church to be the person you've called me to be."'

Joybringers or Joykillers – the Choice Before Us

Matthew 15

by Peter Maiden

PETER MAIDEN

Keswick's current Chairman and International Director of Operation Mobilisation, Peter is a very busy man! He travels extensively to fulfil his commitments with OM – overseeing the day-to-day co-ordination of its ministry in 82 countries worldwide. Peter is also an elder at Hebron Evangelical Church in Carlisle where he lives and manages to include itinerant Bible teaching in the UK and overseas into his schedule. Peter enjoys family life with his wife Win and their three children and grandchildren as well as endurance sports! In particular he loves long-distance running, fell walking and long-distance cycling.

Joybringers or Joykillers – the Choice Before Us

Matthew 15

Introduction

There is a Muslim people group in Algeria, where God is at work in quite exceptional ways. From a very small base, the church has grown rapidly to about forty thousand believers, from Muslim backgrounds. If you want to get into one of their churches, you have to get there at least an hour before the start of the service. We've had teams working down there over the past few years and I've been rejoicing at the reports of what God has been doing.

A few weeks ago I was in Izmir, in Turkey, speaking at a conference for our workers and they brought with them six or seven of the leaders of this movement. Some people are speaking of the movement in terms of revival. I watched these Christian leaders worshipping and do you know something? As they worshipped, they danced and it wasn't just a sort of sanctified shuffle. They were doing the full works, they were circling, they were waltzing and if you know the sort of background that I'm from, you can imagine what a shock that was to my system. I began to dislike myself intensely because I found myself thinking, Can such people, who do such things, possibly be used of God in revival? I was ready, for a few moments at least, to discount all that I'd heard God was doing in this people group, just because of what I saw.

How can we be right before God?

Put my troubles to one side for a moment and come with me to our passage here in Matthew 15. The pressure on Jesus has been increasing now for some time. In Matthew's gospel the record of this pressure begins in chapter 9. 'Some people brought to Jesus a paralysed man and Jesus said to him: "Take heart my child, your sins are forgiven."' Matthew records that the reaction of the teachers of religious law to that was, 'Blasphemy, this man is talking as if he were God.' When Jesus called the author of this gospel to be one of his disciples, Matthew organised a celebration party and his dinner guests included many of his fellow tax collectors and others, whom he himself describes as notorious sinners. Then Matthew records the response of the Pharisees; they were indignant and they asked the disciples of Jesus, 'Why does your teacher eat with such scum?'

Not long after it gets really nasty. After the healing of two blind men and one man who couldn't speak because he was possessed by a demon, their conclusion is this: 'He can cast out demons because he is empowered by the prince of demons.' All the time the pressure is building. And here in chapter 15 it reaches the point of explosion. Some Pharisees and teachers of religious law come all the way from Jerusalem to Galilee, to interview Jesus. That's quite a distance, so it's clear Jesus is now high on the priority list when the Pharisees meet in committee.

I don't think these Pharisees had been to Dale Carnegie's seminar on how to win friends and influence people. Their interview skills certainly seem to lack tact. 'Why do your disciples disobey our age-old traditions? … They ignore our tradition of ceremonial hand washing before they eat.' The response of Jesus appears to be equally lacking in tact. If, as the book of Proverbs tells us, a soft answer turns away wrath, wouldn't that have been a better option for Jesus? But look at his reply. 'And why do you, by your traditions, violate the direct commandments of God?'

Jesus knows there's absolutely no place for negotiation and compromise here. This is not the place to sit down in committee and see if we can find common ground. It's not the time to set up a commission, to report back in three years and see if a common way forward can be reached. No. This is not really a collision between Jesus and the Pharisees. This is a collision between two views of religion. This is the big issue. How can a person be right before God? How can a person enjoy a relationship with him? Here, two answers are being presented. And between these two answers, absolutely no common ground can ever be found.

The traditions of the elders

Let's look at the specific issue for a moment: disobeying age-old tradition and in particular ceremonial hand washing, before they ate. That was their accusation. These age-old traditions, sometimes called the traditions of the elders, refer to a large body of teaching which was largely oral at the time of Jesus. It interpreted the law, often going into great detail of how the law would impact every aspect of your daily life. When this oral teaching was later written down, one entire section dealt just with hands, specifying such details as how much water must be used for effective ceremonial purification. If a man poured water over one hand with a single rinsing, the Rabbis said his hand was clean but if over both hands with a single rising, then Rabbi Mayer declares them unclean unless he pours more than a quarter jug of water over his hands. Minute detail; just one example of how the interpretation of the law of God invaded every area of their lives.

It was absolutely an incredible weight to carry through their lives. It's little wonder that the apostle Paul likens it to the weight of a yoke. Imagine the oxen, nose in the ground, weighed down by the yoke, unable to raise its head. That, says Paul, is the person living under law, bowed down by its weight, unable to lift your head.

It's not that the law was unimportant. In Matthew 5, the great Sermon on the Mount, Jesus makes it clear he did not come to rubbish the law. And Jesus does not suggest that the interpretation of that law, for our daily life, does not require holiness: it certainly does. The holiness required is the inner renewal of our lives but it also meant change in outward conduct. For the Jew, it included ritual obligations, even in this area of washing. We saw that the priests, before performing various sacred duties, had to bathe. Aaron and his sons were ordered to cleanse their hands before performing duties in the tabernacle and, under certain prescribed conditions, the people, in general, had to wash their hands.

So what's wrong with the position of the Pharisees? Can I suggest that they were guilty of three things, which so many have been guilty of, before and since and which I, today, have to be constantly on my guard against. Firstly, they demanded more than God demanded; secondly they demanded far, far less in reality than God demanded and thirdly, they got away from the heart of the matter.

Demanding more than God

There were certain obligations required of the faithful Jew in this area of washing but God's law nowhere required ritual hand cleansing, for everybody, in connection with every meal. That was, absolutely, a tradition of the elders; indeed, it was an addition of the elders. It was not the command of God.

I believe it's a favourite tactic of our enemy to make God appear, to us, much more strict than he actually is. It's a favourite tactic to show God in a negative, demanding light. We can see something of this as far back as the garden of Eden. God's command to Adam was very clear, given in the context of great generosity. 'You can freely eat any fruit in the garden except fruit from the tree of the knowledge of good and evil. If you eat of its fruit, you will surely die.' But when Satan tempts Eve, remember her response, 'God says we must not eat it or even touch it'. Already the simple command is being added to, made more demanding than it actually was.

This was one of the major issues that the early church had to face. Paul and Barnabas are in Antioch and some men from Jerusalem arrive and begin to teach the Christians, 'Unless you keep the ancient Jewish custom of circumcision taught by Moses, you cannot be saved.' Paul and Barnabas forcibly disagree and the result of the disagreement is that Paul and Barnabas are sent to Jerusalem, with some of the local believers and the first great committee meeting of the church takes place.

They stopped off in Phoenicia and Samaria, as they made their way to Jerusalem and they told the believers there of what God had done. This is Luke's account, from the New Living Translation. 'They told them – much to everyone's joy – that the Gentiles, too, were being converted.' That is the result of the work of God. When God is at work, the result is joy.

So they move on to Jerusalem. This is what we read. '... some of the men who had been Pharisees before their conversion stood up and declared that all Gentile converts must be circumcised and be required to follow the law of Moses' (Acts 15:5). What's the one thing lacking in Jerusalem? Joy. Joy thieves, grace killers are at work.

I feel a real compassion for these people. Notice the objectors were those who'd been Pharisees before their conversion. I've watched the struggle that people have, who come to Christ from a strict conservative background, to live in the freedom that Christ bought for us at the cross. It can be an immense and very painful struggle and my heart often goes out to those who are battling with it. But battle they must and stand firm we must because, as we saw earlier on these issues, there can be absolutely no compromise. We are here, at the very heart of the gospel.

Thank God, the Jerusalem leaders didn't compromise, they didn't give an inch to these converted Pharisees and, after the great committee meeting, they sent a letter to the believers. '... it seemed good to the Holy Spirit and to us to lay no greater burden on you than these requirements: You must abstain from eating food offered to idols, from consuming blood or eating the meat of strangled animals, and from sexual immorality' (Acts 15:28,29).

Interesting that they put these food requirements alongside abstinence from sexual immorality. They did that for the purpose of fellowship. It would have been a bit too much for the Jewish believers, if these brand new Gentile believers immediately started trampling under foot all of their eating practices. It reminds us that, in our freedom in Christ, though things may be acceptable, they may not always be expedient. Sometimes we have to handle our wonderful freedom very sensitively, for the purpose of fellowship.

When we read about such things as hand washing requirements, we probably feel, 'We'll never get into anything like that.' But a vital question for us, for me, today, is this: am I in danger of being a grace killer? Could I possibly be a joy thief? I'm not going to get into written laws, adding to the law of God. But do I put expectations on people which go much further than the law of God expects?

A very sad statement about some Evangelicals is that they are people who are awfully worried that someone, somewhere is having fun and they need to repent of it. It reminds me of Mark Twain's words about people who were good, in the worst possible sense of that word.

Some of you may be familiar with the missionary peanut butter story. It's a true story. An American couple were serving in a part of the world where there was no access to peanut butter. They happened to enjoy peanut butter very much so they made arrangements with their friends in the States, to send them a regular supply. They didn't know, until this regular supply began to arrive, that other missionaries at the mission station, considered it a mark of spirituality that they did not have peanut butter with their meals. 'We believe, that since we cannot get peanut butter here, we should give it up for the cause of Christ.' Bearing the cross, for them, was living without peanut butter. But this family didn't buy into that line of thinking and the regular supply of peanut butter kept arriving.

Now they didn't flaunt their peanut butter, I don't actually know how you flaunt peanut butter, but they didn't flaunt their peanut butter. They just ate it in the privacy of their home but the pressure intensified. You would expect missionaries, wouldn't you, to be big enough to allow people to eat whatever they pleased? Yes? No. The legalism actually became so petty, the pressure got so intense, their treatment so unfair, that this couple got to the point that they couldn't take any more. They packed it all in and they came back from the field, disillusioned and, sadly, rather cynical. A modern example of squint-eyed legalists spying out and attacking someone else's liberty. I ask you, how can people like us, who follow the heroes of our faith who are freedom fighters: men like Moses, Abraham, Paul and supremely Jesus himself; how can we ever slip into that deadly form of legalism?

Demanding less than God

God was looking for changed hearts, through his commandments, for radically changed lives. He was looking for change within but the Pharisees had become content with adherence to a rule book.

It's much easier to observe rules and regulations, and it's much easier to check up on those who don't, than it is to pray and to seek for a changed heart, which will result in totally changed attitudes. Legalism rather than love, law rather than relationship, has always been the easier option. But though they insisted on these rules, they constantly changed them, to make them more acceptable, more achievable and Jesus gives a startling example of that here.

Mark's account of the incident is slightly clearer. Jesus says, 'Moses gave you this law from God: "Honor your father and mother," … But you say it is all right for people to say to their parents, "Sorry, I can't help you. For I have vowed to give to God what I could have given to you."'

Here's a person who has parents who are in need, and they've come to their children seeking assistance. In order not to help them by giving them some particular item, all the child has to do is to say either it's a gift or an offering. Really they are saying, 'I've consecrated that to God.' Then the child was immediately released from helping their parents. Jesus is saying, 'You tell us that you're following all these minute commands but you're nullifying the commands of God by your own traditions.' Some children, it appears, went even further and they said, 'Whatever I have that might be of benefit to you, either now or in the future is dedicated to God. Keep your hands off it.'

This is the first time in his ministry that Jesus refers to the Pharisees as hypocrites but he has no other option. This is hypocrisy of the highest order and it wasn't just on one issue they did this kind of thing. Remember in the Sermon on the Mount how often those words 'But I say unto you' occur. The Pharisees were saying this about the law of God but Jesus says, 'I say unto you' because they were constantly changing the true meaning of the law; interpreting it in ways which often appear to be incredibly accurate interpretations, but which actually took away the whole true meaning. Probably, without realising it, the issue became this: 'How little do I need to do to keep the law of God? What's the absolute minimum? I have to love my neighbour, that's clear, but Gentiles, they aren't neighbours, are they?'

That is the great challenge of the story of the good Samaritan. The expert in religious law asks his question, 'What must I do to inherit eternal life?' and Jesus responds, 'What does the law of Moses say?' The lawyer answers, perfectly correctly, 'Love the Lord your God with all your heart, soul, mind, strength and love your neighbour as yourself.' But then we're told, to justify his actions, he asks a supplementary question. 'And who is my neighbour?'

He's trying to limit the definition of neighbour. 'How few people can I actually be obligated to show this love to and still keep the commandment?' But the story Jesus tells challenges him to entirely change his question. Jesus is saying, 'You should be asking, "Who can I possibly be a neighbour to today? Where, today, can I find people who I can show this love to?"'

Again, I have to ask myself; am I ever guilty of this attitude? Rather than a generous, sacrificial, positive approach to my faith, do I become careful? 'I have to give a tithe but is that a tithe of gross or net?' That's probably a very bad example because I think Christian giving a tithe today are probably the generous ones.

So easily we become rule-keepers, rather than joyful, generous, liberal bond-slaves. Maybe that Pauline idea of the bond slave helps. The bond slave was the slave who'd been granted freedom by his master but because of the relationship which had been built between the slave and the master, he doesn't take the opportunity for freedom. He commits to serve, for the remainder of his days. Imagine the difference in the working relationship for the bond slave and the normal slave. For the normal slave, it's a duty, he does what he does because he has to do it and there'll be trouble if he doesn't. But the bond slave is serving because he wants to, this is no duty, this is privilege, his motive is gratitude and love. He's not involved, any longer, in rule-keeping, only relationship.

That was the problem with these Pharisees, they appeared to demand more than God demanded but in reality, they demanded far, far less. And all of this led to a third problem.

Getting away from the heart of the matter

Jesus returned to the sea of Galilee and climbed a hill and sat down. A vast crowd brought him the lame, blind, crippled, mute and many others with physical difficulties, and they laid them before Jesus. And he healed them all. The crowd was amazed! Those who hadn't been able to speak were talking, the crippled were made well, the lame were walking around, and those who had been blind could see again! And they praised the God of Israel' (Mt. 15:29–31).

When you've been reading the Bible for a few years, as I have been, you can get over-familiar with that sort of passage. Here is an utterly incredible scene; the blind can see, the crippled are standing upright, those who couldn't speak are chattering in groups and the lame, no doubt, are dancing. And there were not just one or two examples of this but everyone, at this particular time, brought to Jesus was healed.

No wonder we read 'the crowd was amazed,' no wonder they praised the God of Israel.

But while all this was going around them, what were the Pharisees doing? They were complaining about such things as ceremonial hand washing. And they obviously believed that, because Jesus did not insist that his disciples kept their rules exactly on that matter, he could not possibly be the genuine article. This was enough for them to make him and his whole ministry unauthentic. It didn't matter about the lame dancing, it didn't matter about those who couldn't speak, chattering. 'Your disciples are not washing their hands properly.' Talk about not being able to see the wood for the trees! The Son of God is among them, he's doing things which cause the crowds to praise the God of Israel but the quite miserable and pathetic response of these religious leaders is, 'Can't you get your disciples to wash their hands properly?' Minute incidentals have become so important to them, that they've completely missed the heart of the matter. The Son of God is among them and he's doing his work.

Come back with me to Turkey, to my Algerian friends, waltzing and dancing. What am I going to do? Am I going to say they can't possibly be the real deal? What happened amongst those people can't possibly be true just because they have a different approach at that point?

I find this fifteenth chapter of Matthew a great warning for me. I've seen it over and over again, believers who get hung up on a particular doctrine or practice and that becomes so important to them that they judge everything and everyone by it. It might, for example, be that particular view on how the world began, or how the world will end. And if you don't share their detailed view on that issue, then you're definitely suspect. Or what will proceed the second coming of our Lord. It's very hard for them to see that God can really be working in and through you, if you don't follow what they believe on that particular issue. A popular one today is that if you haven't had the same experience of the Holy Spirit as I have, you must be suspect.

The three great failings of the Pharisees; they appeared to demand more than God demanded, in reality, they demanded far less. And, tragically, their concentration on minute non-essentials caused them to miss the only real essential; the presence and the glory of the Son of God himself.

Matthew drives all of this home for us, first with an illustration and then by the incident he chooses to record next, in the ministry of Jesus. First the illustration: in verses 17 and 18, in layman's language, Jesus says, 'What you eat eventually goes into the toilet. The external observing of all the rules, the signing of all the pledges, the inner spiritual life is not necessarily touched by such things. But what about that which comes from the mouth, comes from within, that's what counts, that's what shows the true you. Out of the heart, come evil thoughts.'

Hendrickson says the word used there has given us the English word 'dialogue', so it's sometimes translated 'out of the heart come schemes, deliberations'. So you're offended by someone, what comes out of your heart? What kind of dialogue do you have with yourself? 'How can I get my own back? How can I get even?' Someone cuts in on you, when you're driving, what kind of dialogue ensues? We will know ourselves, as we answer that question. As so many have put it, the heart of the matter is the matter of the heart.

What's the next incident that Matthew records? Jesus moves about fifty miles, crossing the border line between strictly Jewish and Gentile territory and he meets a Gentile woman. She's outside the ritual of the Jewish covenant, not familiar with all the externals but she has a heart which just will not take 'No' for an answer. Jesus says, 'I was sent only to the people of Israel. One day the mission of the disciples will take them to the Gentiles but not yet. Salvation is from the Jews and to them I must go.' But talk about persistent faith. The women kneels before Jesus, worshipping him and crying, as only the mother of an afflicted child can cry. 'Lord help me, I know I've nothing to offer, I've nothing to plead, I'm outside of the covenants but Lord have mercy, please help me. I may well be a Gentile dog but just a crumb of the uncovenanted mercies of God, is all I ask.' And the faith, the heart that seeks only mercy, is the heart that is honoured. She will receive the blessings of Christ. These Pharisees, they will receive the woes of Christ (when we get to chapter 23).

The heart of the matter, is the matter of the heart. How is your heart, my heart? Is it a heart captured by the love, joy and freedom of Christ? Or is hard, rigid, falsely secure in the safety of rule-keeping?

Philip Yancey, in his beautiful book, *What's so amazing about Grace*, quotes from a column by the humourist, Erma Bombeck.

> In church the other Sunday I was intent on a small child who was turning around smiling at everyone. He wasn't gurgling, spitting, humming, kicking, tearing the hymnals, or rummaging through his mother's handbag. He was just smiling. Finally, his mother jerked him around and in a stage whisper, that could be heard in a little theatre in Broadway said 'Stop that grinning! You're in church!' With that, she gave him a belt and as the tears rolled down his cheeks added, 'That's better,' and returned to her prayers ...
>
> Suddenly I was angry. It occurred to me the entire world is in tears, and if you're not, then you'd better get with it. I wanted to grab this child with the tear-stained face close to me and tell him about my God. The happy God. The smiling God. The God who had to have a sense of humor to have created the likes of us. ... By tradition, one wears faith with the solemnity of a mourner, the gravity of a mask of tragedy and the dedication of a Rotary badge.
>
> What a fool, I thought. Here was a woman sitting next to the only light left in civilisation – the only hope, our only miracle – our only promise of infinity. If he couldn't smile in church, where was there left to go?[1]

Paul exhorts the Galatians, 'Stand fast in your freedom, the freedom with which Christ has set you free.' He says to the Galatians, 'You're no longer slaves, you're sons, you're daughters and, since you're his children, everything he has belongs to you.'

I think the result of all this was intended to be joy and freedom, don't you? Please don't allow the devil to steal our spiritual birthright. And when I meet the dancing Algerians next, pray that I'll dance with them.

---

[10] Philip Yancey, *What's So Amazing About Grace* (Grand Rapids: Zondervan, 1997).

The Challenge of Caring

Matthew 18

by Hugh Palmer

HUGH PALMER

Hugh Palmer is the Minister of Christ Church, Fulwood, in Sheffield. Before that he served as Curate at Holy Trinity Norwich and also at St Helen's, Bishopsgate, in London. He is Director of Northern Cornhill Training College.

The Challenge of Caring

Matthew 18

Introduction

Tell me, do you know any of these characters? Let me try and introduce you. Fred, I've not got a photo of him, but how shall I describe him? Well, he is whatever the PC word for oddball is. If you find yourself trapped into a conversation with Fred, however hard your conscience tells you to stay and talk, all your body language is backing away. Mrs Smith, on the other hand, is a dear but, to put it kindly, she is slow. Worse still, her mind keeps flitting so when she remembers to turn up, it never helps the flow of the home group. She can come up with the strangest of questions or the obscurest of comments.

Peter is as sharp as Mrs Smith is slow; so sharp and clear-cut, that when he's said something, that is it. It's not worth suggesting an alternative, he'll simply fire a question straight at you and you'll look a complete fool because you won't have an answer. Jane; well, to be perfectly honest, between you and me, it is rather difficult thinking that Jane goes on calling herself a Christian. She's a character and she's got a past as well. The men you used to see her around with, they were the least of the problems, to be honest. Certainly, this marriage is lasting, in a way the others didn't and the babies have made a difference but the past still catches up with the present. And she'll drop out of church, for weeks on end, and you know it'll take hours and hours of someone's time to help her find her feet again.

Paul comes from one of those stalwart church families. You've known him since he was knee-high to a grasshopper. You know he can call himself a Christian, all right, it's just that he's always been a rebel. It is not just the way he dresses, it's the ideas he's had. He's always asking awkward questions. He's never willing to buy into our assumptions, he's always got to query them. You know, whether they're moral. 'Why?' 'How can you say that?' 'Why not give to this cause?' And he can't ever do it nicely, it's always got to be aggressive. It's never, 'Don't you think it would be nice to give to this as well?' It's always, 'Why waste your time doing that, when it's perfectly obvious the only sensible thing to do is this?'

What have these characters got in common? They are the sort of folk who, just between you and me, if they didn't turn up, there'd be at least someone who'd heave a sigh of relief and feel it probably doesn't, actually, matter that much. In fact it could be easier without them. And, along with the shrug, the thought might just cross someone's mind, 'There are plenty of others.'

Keep those characters in mind as you open Matthew chapter 18 and we face up to the challenge of this chapter. I think this chapter's written because Jesus knows that people think the way I've just been talking. Christians think that way, church leaders think that way, Keswick Convention-goers think that way. I may not have described the one that provokes that reaction in you but you understand the temptation. When I talk about the challenge of caring, I'm not meaning, 'Will you care?' I take it we've got that far. We know the answer to that question's 'Yes.' It's just the real question is, 'Who will you care for?'

Who will you care for?

This chapter is full of teaching on how the Christian community works and how it ought to relate and right at the heart of it, Jesus tells that very famous little story. Look at it, in verse 12. What do you think? Put yourself in this man's shoes. If a man owns 100 sheep and one of them wanders away, what would you do? Adopt the cost efficiency approach? 'It's a much better use of my time to carry on looking after 99 than go wandering after one...' Make the logical judgement? 'If he chooses to wander off, he must learn that there are consequences.' Or leave the door open a bit? 'If he comes back, we'll welcome him with open arms.' Would grace make a difference? What would grace do?

We know it wouldn't do any of those things because we're not like that. If you've got four children and you discover you've got one missing, what do you do? It was ten years back. Our family and another family of friends did a day trip to Calais and our youngest couldn't have been more than six. We were caught up in a procession and we were wandering along. We thought he was with that family, they thought he was with us and, suddenly, we discover he's missing. What do we do? Gather the other two and say, 'Well, three's always been a handful. Why don't we just stick here?' Of course not. You're worried about this six-year-old, he's in France, he doesn't understand a word of French, can't speak it, where's he gone?

I was delegated to go up to the front of the procession. He must have wandered ahead so I'm looking everywhere, elbowing my way through. I get to the very front row, no sign of him, and that's when it really hits you in the pit of the stomach. I'm going back, still trying to keep half an eye out for him and in my head I'm trying to think, 'What am I going to do when I get back to Clare and the rest and we can't find him? We've got to tell the police. How do I explain to the police in French that the boy's missing? How do I describe in English what he's wearing? I'm a man, I don't notice that kind of thing.' That's what we do when one's missing, isn't it?

'If a man owns a hundred sheep, and one of them wanders away, will he not leave the 99 on the hills and go to look for the one that wandered off? And if he finds it, I tell you the truth, he is happier about that one sheep than about the 99 that did not wander off.' By the time you've searched all round the hills and found the thing, stuck on some silly ledge and got it up again and brought it home – when you've been through all that – with a sheep, you're not going to let it go lightly.

'Well,' says Jesus, 'it's like that, with God.' 'In the same way, your Father in heaven is not willing that any of those little ones should be lost' (verse 14). He is that kind of shepherd, he always has been, as a matter of fact. If you want to read about him, read Ezekiel 34; you'll find he's exactly that kind of shepherd. There really isn't a lot to this parable; it's very straightforward and yet the challenge is very clear. It's a challenge to those of us who are tempted to look down on the Freds, the Mrs Smiths, the Peters, the Janes, the Pauls. His heart breathes a sigh of concern. To those of us who discover someone missing and say, 'Well, not my type. It doesn't matter too much, there are plenty of others'; God is saying, even of those awkward ones, 'Just my type. Couldn't matter more. Where is he? Where is she?'

Let me try and put this question reverently: why does God count sheep? It is not because he's trying to get to sleep. It's because he's got a heart for the stray; he wants to check he's got them all. Why does God count sheep? Because he does not want to lose any. Look again at verse 14. I wonder if there's comfort for someone who feels on the edge, that you don't matter. Look and believe, 'In the same way, your Father in heaven is not willing that any of these little ones should be lost.'

The challenge to those of us who call ourselves Christians is, do we reflect that heart of God? The challenge of caring is not, will we care? But, who will we care for? Or if you learn better when you put it the other way round, the challenge of caring in this chapter is matched with a warning: the danger of despising. 'See that you do not look down on one of these little ones. For I tell you that their angels in heaven always see the face of my Father in heaven' (verse 10). These little ones, it's so easy to look down on.

The danger of despising

The stray sheep are that important. Everything, in this chapter, is warning us about handling our relationships with one another wrongly inside the kingdom community. And the major warning is this one: to look down on a Christian brother or sister. Luke uses the parable of the stray sheep evangelistically, Matthew uses it pastorally. Actually, they may not be that different. Throughout the Bible, there are two major strategies in God's evangelistic thrust. One is the missionary one of being sent and going and the other is God drawing a people to himself. When people live truly as the people of God, it is very attractive. It's the magnet principle. A community that lives the way this chapter describes is massively attractive.

Take some of the examples. Let's take these little ones. The context is there, in the very beginning of the chapter, in verse 1. The little children, in this chapter, represent the Christian believer. And the mark of the little child – it's not that little children are innocent. You don't have to be a parent for very long to work that one out. It isn't even that little children are naturally humble, most are remarkably self-centred, but it is that they're insignificant. They didn't count.

'I want to be the greatest.' 'If that's what you want, then you need to learn to be someone who's a nobody.' He'll say it again, in a couple of chapters' time, 'Whoever wants to be the first needs to be the least. You want to be the greatest, learn to be a slave. Be a nobody.' Tell me, verse 5, what do you do when you're face to face with a nobody? What would grace do? 'Welcome,' says Jesus. '… whoever welcomes a little child like this in my name welcomes me.'

Whose company are we willing to keep? This is a sure test of our self-importance and the little child we're urged to welcome is the Christian, be they three or ninety-three. Are they insignificant because they're a bit odd, like a Fred? Slow, like a Mrs Smith? Awkward, like a Paul? Who knows where, like a Jane? A rebel, like a Paul? Are they a nobody because they've a disability? They just don't count in this community. They're the sort of person that you're having a conversation with but, all the time, you're actually looking for 'the important person.' You'd love to have a conversation over there because that really would matter and this conversation's going nowhere. No, it isn't going anywhere and the whole point of the conversation is not to go anywhere but that it's happening. The significance is that you are having a conversation with someone and it's a way of saying that they do matter and they do belong. But actually, my eyes are all ready for the one I really want to have, with the person who really does matter. Or is it just difficult because it's the person with whom I disagree? 'Their worldview had been so profoundly opposite to mine. The way they've dealt in business has been so profoundly damaging. Their sexual orientation, their sexual history's anathema to me and now I'm face to face with someone I disagree with and how on earth am I meant to relate?'

I was reading the story of Chuck Colson, the founder of Christian Prison Fellowship, which is a remarkable work bringing the gospel to prisoners right round the world. Chuck Colson was the right-hand man to President Nixon. He was his hatchet man, a ruthless lawyer, caught up in the cover-up of Watergate. He got charged over that and later convicted and sentenced. And in between being charged and coming to trial, Chuck Colson was converted. A friend of his, a man called Doug Coe, tried to arrange a meeting with a senior Christian senator, Harold Hughes. When Doug Coe called Harold Hughes and asked him if he'd meet with Chuck Colson, Hughes said, 'There isn't anyone I dislike more than Chuck Colson. I'm against everything he stands for.' Before Hughes hung up, Doug gently suggested that the senator's attitude was hardly Christ-like. The next day, Hughes called back and relented. So they had the meeting.

Colson wasn't prepared when Hughes put him centre stage. 'Chuck, they tell me you've had an encounter with Jesus Christ. Would you tell us about it?' Colson said, 'I wasn't ready to talk about Christ to a room full of people I hardly knew and the words came out haltingly. But, to my surprise, there was no embarrassment, simply a feeling of inadequacy in talking about the most intimate experience of my life. In the middle, I almost bogged down, as I wondered, "Are they going to think I'm some kind of nut? Do people really go around talking about their personal encounters with God?" I stopped, momentarily, looked around the room and no one spoke but their expressions told me to keep going.' And, when he'd finished, there was silence. Colson goes on, 'Harold Hughes, whose face had been enigmatic while I talked, suddenly lifted both hands in the air and brought them down, hard, on his knees. "That's all I need to know, Chuck," he said. "You've accepted Jesus, he's forgiven you. I do the same. I love you now as my brother in Christ. I'll stand with you, I'll defend you anywhere and I'll trust you with anything I have."' Colson said, 'I was overwhelmed, so astonished that I could only utter a feeble "Thank you." In all my life, no one had ever been so warm and loving to me outside of my family. And now it was coming from a man who had loathed me for years and whom I'd known for barely two hours.' Colson's a bear of a man, a ruthless lawyer but he was a little one.

'… whoever welcomes a little child like this in my name welcomes me.' What would grace do? Welcome, not trip up. '… if anyone causes one of these little ones who believe in me to sin, it would be better for him to have a large millstone hung around his neck and to be drowned in the depths of the sea' (verse 6). I always used to think that verse had to refer to some appalling abuse or leading into gross immorality and it certainly includes that. But it must also include that cold shouldering that will stop the little child from growing in Christ and push someone beyond the margins. The way Jesus speaks reminds us that this encouragement, to show the grace of welcome, belongs in the kingdom file. It's that serious.

What would grace do?

Turn on, verse 15: 'If your brother sins against you,' well, avoid him for a bit and make sure no one else gets hurt by him, let them know what he's done? What would grace do? '… go and show him his fault, just between the two of you. If he listens to you, you have won your brother over.' Grace will try to win over. It'll happen; the mark of the kingdom community is not that we're all perfect, so we really don't need to go on pretending we are to one another. It's actually how we handle the offence. Wrongs are faced, they're not ignored. The wronged brother or sister has a responsibility here, to take deliberate action; not to hide in a trench, not to grumble to friends, but to win over, not to put down. And if you go to show him his fault, please do remember that's why you're going. Not to make all the points you've had brewing up but to win over. It doesn't come easily. That's why Jesus teaches like this, and if ever someone comes to you to explain how you've offended, please listen sensitively. I know we all think we're the most approachable people but actually, for people to come and say, 'Brother, you have offended me', it often takes a huge effort. They've screwed themselves up and the words come out wrong and they're tense and it gets aggressive, in a way it wasn't meant to be. I need to learn to listen, to show the grace my way, that he or she is trying to win me over.

Here's the mark of a grace community, it doesn't pretend there are no faults, it doesn't put down behind the back, it faces up to it, it wants to win over.

It doesn't always happen. 'But if he will not listen, take one or two others along, so that "every matter may be established by the testimony of two or three witnesses" (verse 16). That's often helpful, if there's someone else who can interpret in all the static that's going on. 'If he refuses to listen to them, tell it to the church; and if he refuses to listen even to the church, treat him as you would a pagan or a tax collector.' There may need to be discipline, there is behaviour that is unacceptable to this family life but it is less the original fault, notice, nor the refusal to face it, but the refusal to engage with grace.

What would grace do, if a brother offends you? Seek to win over, not put down. And when the fault is faced, when the wronged person is listened to, when repentance comes and apology is offered, what would grace do then? Forgive.

So when Peter comes to Jesus, he's ahead of the game. He's worked it out. 'I've gone to him, I've told him his offence, he's repented, I've forgiven. And, lo and behold, next week, he's gone and done something similar again and I go to him and he repents and I forgive and it happens again, a month later and a month later. How many times do I do it, Lord, until I'm just being taken for a ride?' It's a good question. 'Up to seven times?'

What would grace do? The moment you start counting, you've got it wrong, you've missed the point. Don't get your calculator out: '75… 76… one more then I'll have him.'

No. 'I tell you, not seven times, 77 times.' I don't know whether we understand what a hugely powerful weapon forgiveness is and what an endlessly commonplace thing it is.

A preacher preached a sermon on forgiveness. And a lawyer came, thanked him for the message and added, 'I'm not a Christian. I've never accepted this idea of the innocent suffering for the guilty. This blood religion,' as he put it. And the preacher said to him, 'Sir, I'm very sorry; you can't have a happy marriage or a happy family or any lasting friendships.' The lawyer said, 'Why not?' The preacher replied, 'Because you're not an angel and you make mistakes. And the only way in which people can keep on accepting you is if they, as innocent, will forgive your guilt and accept you but you just told me you don't believe in the innocent suffering for the guilty.' Do you realise how devastating it is to relationships, if forgiveness is what we don't exercise?

What would grace do? Forgive; but it's not just that grace forgives, it will forgive and not stand firm.

I know it's a bit of a shock, so please listen carefully. There are things to stand firm on. The uniqueness of Jesus Christ, as God's only Lord and Saviour, don't budge an inch but what is your due and what are your rights? Forgive, don't stand firm.

The cost of forgiveness

Jesus tells another story, to illustrate the point. 'Therefore,' he says, in verse 23, 'the kingdom of heaven is like a king who wanted to settle accounts with his servants. As he began the settlement, a man who owed him ten thousand talents was brought to him.' Now, it all depends which footnote you read, as to how many millions is the equivalent today of 10,000 talents. It's an awful lot of debt. It can be done, presumably, but you have to work at it, to run up this kind of debt. 'Since he was not able to pay, (big surprise) the master ordered that he and his wife and his children and all that he had be sold to repay the debt.' You're not going to get an awful lot for a slave and his family but the whole point is to emphasis the servant's plight. 'The servant fell on his knees before him. "Be patient with me," he begged, "and I will pay back everything."'

A likely story; I don't know how many weeks in a row he'd have to win the National Lottery jackpot to pay it off but more than is ever going to happen. 'The servant's master took pity on him, cancelled the debt and let him go.' It wasn't financial restructuring: 'cancelled'. Put yourself in the servant's shoes for a moment, face up to the reality of the ruin that lies ahead. Recapture the wonder of grace. We take it for granted that God forgives, that's his job. That is so to misunderstand grace. Think of the traffic warden. You've parked on the double yellow line, the traffic warden's got his notebook out. Do you smile and say to your friends, 'It doesn't matter, he'll forgive, it's his job'? Traffic wardens are not paid to act like that. They're paid to act the law, not grace.

This man is staring ruin in the face. 'Cancelled', the relief, the astonishment, the joy, the wonder, the amazing mercy. 'But when that servant went out, he found one of his fellow-servants who owed him a hundred denarii' … Nothing. 'He grabbed him and began to choke him. "Pay back what you owe me!" he demanded. His fellow-servant fell to his knees and begged him, "Be patient with me, and I will pay you back."' Notice the identical words he used a few moments earlier. You'd think it would bring back memories but it doesn't seem to. 'But he refused. Instead, he went off and had the man thrown into prison until he could pay the debt' – and we're shocked. So are the servants. 'When the other servants saw what had happened, they were greatly distressed and went and told their master everything that had happened'… and the king is shocked. 'Then the master called the servant in. "You wicked servant," he said, "I cancelled all that debt of yours because you begged me to. Shouldn't you have had mercy on your fellow-servant just as I had on you?"' And you suspect, as you read verse 34, that too late the unforgiving servant is shocked. 'In anger his master turned him over to the jailers to be tortured, until he should pay back all he owed.'

So understand that this act of grace, it's not in the nice file. It's in the kingdom file; it's that urgent. I remember, some years back, doing a school assembly and I did the Riding Lights version of this unforgiving servant. It's loads of fun and yet you don't miss the punchline. Look at it, verse 35, 'This is how my heavenly Father will treat each of you unless you forgive your brother from your heart.' You wheel round at the end of that sketch and the finger points at the kids in the hall. The kids loved it because they loved all the fun earlier on and as we were going off the stage, the headmaster said to me, 'I'd like to see you in my study in a few minutes please.'

It doesn't matter how old you are, does it? The headmaster's study; it's like police cars going past you on the street, you immediately think, 'What have I done wrong?' I thought, 'He's rumbled it; the head's actually understood the parable, he's seen the sting in the tail and I've had it.' I got into the study and I waited and he came in and wanted to talk about something else completely. He hadn't spotted it at all, just like Jesus had said in chapter 13, 'Though seeing, they do not see; though hearing they do not hear or understand.' But you do understand the parable, you do get it, you have been given the secrets of the kingdom, you do know that God means what he says.

You hate people who live with one rule for the rich and another for the poor. You don't want to live with one rule for yourself and another for others. We don't want to be the kind of people who relate to God by grace and relate to others by ungrace. I hope we don't because God doesn't either and God won't. So we'll discover we can't.

You say, 'How do you square this severity of God with the language of forgiveness?' Only with great difficulty because forgiveness is very costly. Some of you will know the story of the businessman, who'd gone off on the business trip and he'd had an affair. The guilt of it got too much for him and one day, he sat down with his wife and confessed what he'd done. There were tears and questions and angry words and, at the end of it all, tears streaming down her face, his wife said to him, 'I forgive you.' The man could hardly believe it, his bags were packed and he was ready to go and his heart was so light at the thought, he was thrilled, overwhelmed. He went to work the next day, had a meeting that ended early and thought, 'I'll go home early, I'll get some flowers, I'll have a surprise.' He was still so thrilled that he was forgiven. He bought the flowers, went through the door, couldn't find his wife anywhere, then heard a voice upstairs. And, as he started going up the stairs, flowers in hand, he suddenly realised the voice was coming from their bedroom. The darkest of thoughts crossed his mind. He tiptoed across the landing and peered in, because the door was ajar. He heard his wife talking and he saw her, kneeling by the bed. She was praying and she was saying, 'Lord, I find it so hard to forgive.'

There's no one better to speak to about the cost of forgiveness than the Lord. By the time Matthew's story's out, he's faced a kangaroo court, he's been mocked, spat on, whipped and nailed to a cross and, above all, he's experienced 'My God, my God, why have you forsaken me?' Just so he could offer forgiveness.

I speak as a pastor and experience tells me it is very unlikely that I'm only speaking to myself. There will be many of us for whom living by grace, as those who've received and give grace, is not a thing that comes naturally. Jesus giving all this teaching suggests to me that, for each and every one of us, this is an issue, and if you're not aware of it, it may be all the more important an issue for you. What would grace do? Welcome, win over, forgive.

Greatness in the Kingdom of Heaven

Matthew 20:17–28

by John Risbridger

JOHN RISBRIDGER

Growing up in a Christian home, John grew into an active faith at a young age and his mid teens and student years were a time of particular spiritual growth. He joined UCCF in 1994 after five years in hospital management. For six years he led the Southern Team of UCCF before spending four years in the role of Head of Student Ministries. He is now a minister of Above Bar Church in Southampton. John serves as a Trustee of the Keswick Convention. He is married to Alison and they have two daughters. He loves hill walking and plays squash rather badly. Best known to people in Keswick as a music and worship leader, John also has a lifelong love of classical music.

Greatness in the Kingdom of Heaven
Matthew 20:17–28

Introduction

Jesus said, '... whoever wants to become great among you must be your servant, and whoever wants to be first must be your slave'.

Would you say that you want to be great in the kingdom of God? Would you think it was right to aspire to greatness within the kingdom? I have spent the last ten years of my life working with students in university and college Christian Unions. Like any other group of Christians, CUs have their share of problems and frustrations so I don't want to paint an unrealistic and romanticised picture to you. However, time and again I have found myself deeply challenged to meet in Christian Unions young Christian women and men – I put it in that order not for the sake of political correctness but because I have met so many outstanding Christian women – who don't want to scrape through their lives as Christians and get to the grave still just about trusting Jesus, but who really want their lives to count in the kingdom and the purposes of God.

I think of a girl I knew as a student in Reading. She is a great linguist and now lives in a tiny little village, miles away from anywhere, in Tanzania. She has devoted her life to translating the word of God into the local languages there.

I think of a young man who organised a mission that I spoke at in London in January. I remember sitting with him in coffee bars and sensing in him this restless determination that, whatever it would cost, his friends and others who were studying with him in his college were going to hear the good news of Jesus. His motivation was so strong it could almost be intimidating; he was so determined that the good news should be heard.

I remember another young woman, who was very sensitive to global issues, particularly issues of global justice. While she was studying and after graduating, she used her spare time to set up a national network to bring those issues to the attention of students and young graduates and she has lived very sacrificially ever since, in order to keep that network going. Then I think of another young man, coming to me after a CU meeting, saying that God had been calling him to long-term mission in Colombia and he knew that he had to do something about it that evening.

Again and again, over these last ten years, people like this, without even knowing it and certainly without setting out to do it, have challenged me with the strength, clarity and sharpness of their spiritual ambition and determination. They have forced me to ask the question of myself: 'For me has obedience to Christ become something that always has to fit around being able to pay the mortgage at the end of the month? Has it been domesticated? Has it been toned down? Have I lost that zeal, that clarity of purpose and ambition? Am I succumbing to a spiritual version of middle-age spread?'

I think there is a danger that we approach Jesus' words that I have read to you as if he actually intended them to be the graveyard of spiritual ambition. 'If anyone wants to be great among you,' he says, 'he must become your servant and whoever wants to be first must be your slave.' And we imagine that perhaps what Jesus is saying to us is, 'You want to be great in the kingdom, well, what a terrible idea. What naked ambition. What shameless selfishness. How ungodly, how immature.'

But is that what Jesus is really saying? What about losing our lives for Jesus in order that we may find them? What about, as Paul says, running in such a way as to win the prize? What about David who 'served the purpose of God in his generation'? What about Paul calling us to 'beat our bodies and make them our slaves so that we might not be disqualified from the prize'? Jesus didn't say, 'If you want to be great in the kingdom, then pull yourself together and stop it!'

No, he said: '... whoever wants to become great among you must be your servant, and whoever wants to be first must be your slave'. His point was not that the disciples wanted greatness too much, but that they had misunderstood the nature of true greatness in the kingdom of God.

A few weeks back, the US presidential candidate, Senator John Kerry, made international headlines when he announced that Senator John Edwards, his former rival for the Democratic nomination, was to become his running mate in the forthcoming presidential elections in the autumn. I suppose the gravitas and experience of Senator Kerry together with the charisma, personal touch and youthful enthusiasm of John Edwards was going to be the 'dream team' that would somehow woo Middle America for the Democrats and bring the White House back within their grasp. And the papers seem to be saying that Edwards has brought a certain spark and humanity into the Democrats campaign. But, of course, Senator John Edwards hasn't become the running mate of John Kerry simply for love. It's not just because they happen to be good friends. No, there is a promise of high office and a great reward for him because the closer he is to the future President, if future President he becomes, the higher will be his position when he takes over. So, if the campaign is successful and John Kerry does become President, John Edwards will be Vice-President Edwards, no less.

What's in it for me?

In chapters 19 and 20 of Matthew, there is something similar going on among Jesus' inner circle of disciples: Peter, James and John. They have been his closest friends from the start of his public ministry; his running mates in his travels. But things are beginning to reach a rather critical stage, 'When Jesus had finished saying these things, he left Galilee and went into the region of Judea to the other side of the Jordan' (Mt.19:1).

Jesus is leaving Galilee and moving south into Judea and then he is going up to Jerusalem from where the great kings of the past had reigned over Israel. By the time we get to chapter 21, we have Jesus making his triumphal entry into the city and being hailed by the crowds as the King. Things are becoming critical. If Jesus is about to take power, to come into his kingdom, what do Peter, James and John think? They want to make sure that when Jesus comes into his kingdom, he will guarantee them high office. They may have been nobodies in first century society but they have understood that if Jesus is on the brink of power at last, they are on the brink of greatness with him. But their problem is that they have misunderstood the nature of true greatness – just as they have misunderstood the nature of the kingdom itself.

Look at Peter, who thought that greatness was something to be earned. For Peter, as ever direct and frank, the whole question is rather simple. Peter says to Jesus, 'We have left everything to follow you! What then will there be for us?'(Mt. 19:27). Peter and his friends have done Jesus quite a few favours; they've left home, left family, left security, left their businesses in order to follow Jesus and it hasn't escaped Jesus' notice that they've done all these favours for him, has it? 'Now,' says Peter, 'Jesus, it's soon going to be payback time, isn't it? You owe us a thing or two so I'm sure you'll look after our interests. There'll be something for us in your kingdom.'

Peter has just witnessed the discussion between Jesus and the rich young ruler, earlier in chapter 19 and, as far as Peter is concerned, he is not a bit like the rich young ruler, who for all his religious and moral pretensions wasn't willing to give up his riches to follow Jesus. Peter wasn't anything like that at all because Peter had given up everything to follow Jesus. But Peter was not as different to that first century yuppie as he thought he was. After all, what was the rich young ruler's initial approach to Jesus? He comes to Jesus and says,

'Teacher, what good thing must I do to get eternal life?' (Mt. 19:16). For all its sophistication, the religion of the rich young ruler was very simple. You do certain things that God likes and he will give you eternal life in exchange. It's simple.

And yet, what Jesus calls him to is the abandonment of all that he has built up for himself and to cast himself wholly on the mercy of God. For, as Jesus affirms in 19:26, human effort can never achieve salvation. Jesus says, 'With man this is impossible, but with God all things are possible.' As someone once put it, this man's religion was the religion that seeks to do God a favour but what he needed was the religion that would seek the favour of God.

Peter's mindset is actually the same. 'We've done you a favour Jesus. Now what will there be for us?'

Jesus responds.

> I tell you the truth, at the renewal of all things, when the Son of Man sits on his glorious throne, you who have followed me will also sit on twelve thrones, judging the twelve tribes of Israel. And everyone who has left houses or brothers or sisters or father or mother or children or fields for my sake will receive a hundred times as much and will inherit eternal life (Mt.19:28,29).

God is no man's debtor. We will never out-give him. Whatever the sacrifices are that we may make in our lives and in our ministry, God will never owe us anything.

Those who follow Jesus will share in his reign (verse 29) and receive many, many blessings from the kingdom. But, Jesus says to Peter, 'Your mindset is all wrong' (verse 30) ... 'many who are first will be last, and many who are last will be first.' The blessings of the kingdom don't flow to those who, like that rich young ruler, think that they can put God in a position where he owes them something. Instead the blessings of the kingdom flow to those who receive the kingdom like little children, because 'the kingdom of heaven belongs to such as these' (Mt. 19:14). And that's the point.

Do you think that God owes you anything? Do you think that he owes you salvation, a place in heaven, because of your good works, because of your religious observance? Or maybe you understand that it's not like that but you think that he owes you recognition and acclaim in his kingdom for your outstanding service and sacrifice?

If we think that, we deceive ourselves. God owes us nothing. We have nothing but what we have received. The kingdom is a kingdom of grace. We enter the kingdom by the free gift of God's grace. We live in the kingdom by the free gift of his grace which he renews constantly to us and we receive all the blessings and the rewards and the affirmations of the kingdom solely by his grace, by his overwhelming kindness. We never put God in a position where he owes us something.

We evangelical Christians are perhaps a little less likely to make the mistake of the rich young ruler and imagine that it's what we do that will get us into a right relationship with God. We know that that's not right. But is it not the case that so often we imagine we are saved by the grace of the gospel and that we continue in the Christian life by our good works, through which we imagine that we earn God's approval, access to God even? The truth is that this kingdom is grace, grace, grace from start to finish. All our service, all our sacrifice, all we give to the Lord, will never put God in a position where he owes us anything. No, even his rewards are rewards that he gives as gifts of his grace to us. And that's what Peter needed to learn.

What about James and John? They also misunderstood the nature of true greatness because they imagined that greatness was about position and power (Mt. 20: 20–28).

You might imagine, from chapter 19, that Peter had blown it a little bit. As was typical for Peter, he blurted something out and Jesus had to redirect him. But Peter wasn't the only person in Jesus' inner circle and here is the perfect opportunity, with Peter having been put down, for James and John to get in there in front of Peter, who is still trying to process what Jesus has said. But they decide to take a rather different tack. They'll get their mum to ask for them! After all, it's natural enough for a mum to have ambitions for her boys but it was James and John who put her up to it. They also decide to choose their moment carefully. They decide to make their pitch as Jesus sets out for Jerusalem which is to be the place where he will come into his kingdom.

So, reading from verse 17 of chapter 20

> ... as Jesus was going up to Jerusalem, he took the twelve disciples
> aside and said to them, 'We are going up to Jerusalem, and the Son of
> Man will be betrayed to the chief priests and the teachers of the law.
> They will condemn him to death and will turn him over to the Gentiles
> to be mocked and flogged and crucified. On the third day he will be
> raised to life!' Then the mother of Zebedee's sons came to Jesus with
> her sons and, kneeling down, asked a favour of him. 'What is it you
> want?' he asked. She said, 'Grant that one of these two sons of mine
> may sit at your right and the other at your left in your kingdom.'

Isn't that so ugly? Hadn't they heard what Jesus had just said to
them? How can they possibly be preoccupied with their own power
and position when Jesus has just told them that he is on the way to the
cross to be killed? Had they completely ignored what he had said?

James and John had become intoxicated with thoughts of power.
And the desire for power doesn't only corrupt (as Lord Acton so
famously observed) it also blinds us because it so takes over our
world; everything else gets blocked out. Once we become preoccupied with questions of power and authority, we can easily justify
any sin that we may commit. We can overlook any implications of our
actions and ignore the needs and concerns of anyone else because it's
our position that's at stake and that's what matters. And if it runs
unchecked, that desire for power is so desperately destructive, tearing apart families, organisations, ministries, even churches. James
and John had to learn that, in the kingdom of God, true greatness is
not tied to power or to position. Instead, Jesus explains to us the two
marks of true greatness.

The mark of suffering

True greatness is marked by suffering. Jesus says, 'You don't know
what you are asking ... Can you drink the cup I am going to drink?'
(verse 22). Can you hear the sadness in Jesus' voice? These people
that he had spent all this time with have so misunderstood the true

nature of the kingdom. They totally missed out on what he had just said to them. They had ignored it. Sadness perhaps too, because he knew what it would cost these men to be great in the kingdom, even though they had no idea.

The cup that Jesus refers to is the cup of God's wrath. It's a reference to the suffering that Jesus is shortly to endure on the cross and what Jesus is saying is simple. Those who would sit at his table with him in the place of honour in the kingdom will also have to drink from the cup that he drinks from.

James and John think that greatness in the kingdom will be about position, power, prestige and honour. Jesus says, 'It will be about suffering and sacrifice' and so it was for James and for John and, indeed for Peter. James was executed by Herod. John was banished to Patmos. And according to tradition, Peter was crucified upside-down for his Lord.

This week we have heard a lot about the call to suffer. It is a theme to which the Scriptures frequently return. But have we taken this message to heart, to the extent that the next time we are called to suffer in our service of God, we won't be quite so surprised as we were last time? True greatness in the kingdom is not about being recognised. It's not about having power, position, being in the limelight but it's recognised by a willingness to suffer for Jesus. That's the mark of true greatness in the kingdom.

What might that suffering be? Many things; perhaps it might be the sacrifices of a demanding ministry that you do in your spare time when exhausted. The sacrifices involved in the workplace of making a stand from truth and justice and suffering for it in terms of your job or career. Perhaps it might be the pain of mistreatment by others, sometimes even other believers, sadly. And in many contexts, this suffering is concerned with the blatant hostility of an unbelieving world. It can be very painful. But we should not be surprised. Jesus told us this it what it would be to be great in the kingdom. This is what life in the kingdom is like, as Peter himself would later write. 'To this you were called, because Christ suffered for you, leaving you an example, that you should follow in his steps' (1 Pet. 2:21).

Is it not the case that so often it is those times when the Lord calls us to suffer in some way for him that we find ministry blossoming and fruitfulness emerging? I heard, over this last year, of one of our Christian Union groups in Central London. The details of the story are slightly hazy in my mind but, essentially, they have been prevented from meeting in the university buildings and have faced an enormous amount of opposition from the Students' Union there. What has been their response? It's been wonderful. Here was a group who have begun to understand that opposition and suffering are part of the package when it comes to life in the kingdom of God. They prayed and kept on with evangelism. I was talking to the team leader for the area recently and he was telling me about the consequences of what they have done. He says, 'As a result of all this opposition we now have a CU which is far more prayerful, far more active evangelistically, and other colleges all over London are being spurred on in their evangelism because of the suffering.' Isn't it so often the case that when the Lord calls us to suffering, he does make that suffering fruitful? Suffering is one of the marks of true greatness.

The mark of service

The second mark of true greatness that Jesus puts to them is the mark of service. Verse 24, 'When the ten heard about this, they were indignant with the two brothers.' Isn't that what happens when people get interested in power? Have you noticed how divisive it is, how easily we fall out? Of course the other ten were indignant at James and John's reaction.

Then verse 25, 'Jesus called them together and said, "You know that the rulers of the Gentiles lord it over them, and their high officials exercise authority among them".' Just get these words because they could not be clearer from the lips of the Lord Jesus. He says, 'Not so with you.' Or, 'Among you it shall not be so.' Have you got that? Among the rulers of the Gentiles, they lord it over them, and their high officials exercise authority over them, but *among you it shall not be so*. Rather, anyone who wants to become great among you must be your servant and 'whoever wants to be first must be your slave.'

How many of our troubles, how many of my troubles are actually connected up with issues of authority and power? Who will call the shots? I think of some of the heartache I could have saved myself if I had taken Jesus' words to heart more quickly. So many of our discussions of leadership, of roles, of position – in the end they boil down to this. Yet, Jesus said it's completely the wrong paradigm for thinking about how things work in the kingdom. Could he be clearer? 'Among you it shall not be so.' Authority, power, this is not the paradigm for thinking about life and relationships in the kingdom. Instead, he says, true greatness is in service and whoever wants to be first must be your slave.

Those who are great in the kingdom are not those who get all the limelight, those who get the top positions but those who put themselves in the low positions in order to serve God's people and fulfil his purposes.

What's it like to be a servant? It's about not tearing things down in order to get our way but building God's people up in order to fulfil his purpose. It's about not seeking the applause of the beautiful people but supporting and helping the broken and struggling ones. It's about not seeking the limelight but using God's gifts for his glory and for the benefit of the whole of the Christian community, rather than for your own adulation. It's about not making clones of you as you try and minister to and disciple other people but rather helping people not so much to follow you as to follow Christ himself. This is greatness in the kingdom, greatness which takes the lowly path and which serves the people of God.

But of course, this whole section we are looking at begins and ends not with talk of us but with talk of Jesus who is, himself, the model of the very greatness that he had been describing; Jesus the suffering servant, Jesus the King of the kingdom. This is the Jesus who submits himself to suffering. It's clear that Jesus knew exactly what awaited him as he made his way to Jerusalem (Mt. 20:17–19). He knew that there would be the cross and the agony that he would endure and yet resolutely he walks on to die. Verse 17, '… as Jesus was going up to Jerusalem, he took the twelve disciples aside and said to them, "We are going up to Jerusalem, and the Son of Man will be betrayed to the chief priests and the teachers of the law. They will condemn him to death and will turn him over to the Gentiles to be mocked and flogged and crucified. On the third day he will be raised to life!"'

Here is the world's Creator, betrayed, condemned, mocked, flogged, crucified by his creation. Do you feel the force of those passive verbs as he chooses the place of the victim? A single word from his mouth could have destroyed them all in an instant and yet he chooses to go on, determined to fulfil the purposes of the Father. He chooses to submit to suffering. As Paul put it so famously in Philippians 2, he 'made himself nothing, taking the very nature of a servant ... he humbled himself and became obedient to death – even death on a cross' (Phil. 2:7,8). Jesus submits to suffering.

'… whoever wants to be first must be your slave – just as the Son of Man did not come to be served, but to serve, and to give his life as a ransom for many' (Mt. 20:27,28). Why did Jesus choose to submit to suffering? He did it to serve us. The idea of a ransom described here is the idea of a sum of money that must be paid for a prisoner to be released, and we are the prisoners, guilty before a Holy God, facing his just judgement and condemnation for our rebellion against our Creator. We are the prisoners. And the ransom that must be paid is nothing other than the life of the perfect Son of God who gives himself, paying the ransom in order to secure our freedom. He dies in our place the death that we deserve to die. He takes upon himself and into himself the judgement that should have fallen upon us. He pays the price that we could never have paid ourselves. So he secures our freedom, freedom from judgement, to know and love God, to live, to belong in the kingdom.

For all of us, this communion service is a time to allow ourselves again to be broken before the cross of Jesus, realising the price that he has paid, the suffering he endured, the depth of which we never fully will understand. He submitted to suffering, he served us in his suffering. This is what true greatness in the kingdom actually looks like.

We might think that if true greatness is marked by suffering and service then we don't want it. I suspect that's how James and John and Peter reacted, initially. But once we see it in its context here, we realise that the call to true greatness is in fact nothing other than the call to follow Jesus and be like him; he who suffers, who serves, who calls us to follow him.

You may have read of the death yesterday of Francis Crick, the famous geneticist, who with his colleague James Watson discovered the shape of the DNA molecule. Without doubt their work was groundbreaking and hugely significant to the modern science of genetics. But *The Times* reported that, on making the discovery, Crick and his colleague claimed that they had found the secret of life. Francis Crick went on to write the following. 'You, your joys, your sorrows, your memories, your ambitions, your sense of personal identity and free will are in fact no more than the behaviour of a vast assembly of nerve cells and their associated molecules.' That's the secret of life. Did you get it?

If that is the best that atheism can do to describe to us the secret of life, why are we so intimidated? For we are not merely machines or animals. We were made for God to know him, to love him, to obey him joyfully. The secret of life is not the shape of the DNA molecule. The secret of life is the kingdom of God. For that is the treasure hidden in a field. That is the pearl of great price for which we sell everything that we have that we may buy it.

So let me urge you not to settle for mere survival in the kingdom; hanging on half-heartedly to a bit of religion in the hope that one day you can crawl into your grave, just about still a Christian. Instead, let us pursue the greatness of the kingdom, which is true greatness, as we follow the suffering Servant King who went to the cross for us and who calls us to walk the way of the cross as we follow him.

Keswick
ministries
bringing the Word alive

Keswick Ministries was set up in response to demand to take the excellent Bible teaching of the three week summertime Lake District Keswick Convention and make it available throughout the year and around the world. Its work is aimed at Christians of all backgrounds who have a desire to learn from God's Word and let it change their lives.

Keswick Ministries is committed to achieving its aims by:

- providing Bible based training courses for church leaders, youth workers and young people, preachers and teachers, and all those who want to develop their skills and learn more
- promoting the use of books, tapes, videos and CDs so that Keswick's teaching ministry is brought to a wider audience at home and abroad
- producing TV and radio programmes so that superb Bible talks can be broadcast to you at home
- publishing up-to-date details of Keswick's exciting news and events on our website so that you can access material and purchase Keswick products on-line
- publicising Bible teaching events in the UK and overseas so that Christians of all ages are encouraged to attend 'Keswick' meetings closer to home and grow in their faith
- putting the residential accommodation of the Convention Centre at the disposal of churches, youth groups, Christian organisations and many others, at very reasonable rates, for holidays and outdoor activities in a stunning location

If you'd like more details please look at our website (www.keswickministries.org) or contact the General Director by post, email or telephone.

Keswick Ministries, PO Box 6, Keswick, Cumbria, CA12 4GJ, (Tel: 017687 80075), email centre@keswickconv.com

Keswick 2004
Tapes, Videos, CDs and Books

All talks recorded at Keswick 2004, plus many more audio and
video recordings of talks from the Keswick Convention dating back
to 1957 can be ordered from www.iccspreadingtheword.com

Catalogues and price lists of audio tapes of the Keswick Convention
platform and seminar ministry, including much that is not included
in this book, can be obtained from
ICC
Silverdale Road
Eastbourne
BN20 7AB
Tel 01323 643341
Fax 01323 649240
www.iccspreadingtheword.com
Details of videos and CDs of selected sessions can also be obtained
from the above address.
Some previous annual Keswick volumes (all published by STL/
Authentic Media) can be obtained from:
The Keswick Convention Centre, Skiddaw Street, Keswick,
Cumbria, CA12 4BY
phone: 017687 80075
website: www.keswickministries.org
or from your local Christian bookseller or direct from the
publishers, Authentic Media, PO Box 300, Kingstown Broadway,
Carlisle, Cumbria, CA3 0QS, UK.
01228 512512

www.wesleyowen.com

Keswick 2005

Week 1 16th – 22nd July
Week 2 23rd – 29th July
Week 3 30th July – 5th August

The annual Keswick Convention takes place in the heart of the English Lake District, an area of outstanding natural beauty. It offers an unparalleled opportunity for listening to gifted Bible exposition, meeting Christians from all over the world and enjoying the grandeur of God's creation. Each of the three weeks has a series of morning Bible readings, and then a varied programme of seminars, lectures, literary lunches, prayer meetings, concerts/drama and other events throughout the day, with evening meetings that combine worship and teaching. There is also a full programme for children and youth, and a special track for those with learning difficulties which takes place in week 2. K2, the interactive track for those in their twenties and thirties, also takes place in week 2.

The theme for Keswick 2005 is 'The Glory of the Gospel' and speakers confirmed so far are:

Sinclair Ferguson from Westminster Theological Seminary, Dallas (who will give the Bible readings in week 1); Reverend Stephen Gaukroger of Goldhill Baptist Church (who will give the Bible readings in week 2) and Dominic Smart of Gilcomston South Church (who will give the week 3 Bible readings). Other speakers will include Brother Andrew, Robert Amess, Steve Brady, David Cook, Elaine Duncan, Dave Fenton, Liam Goligher, Mark Greene, Jonathan Lamb, Peter Maiden, Joe Stowell, Rob Whittaker and Keith White.

For further information, please contact:

The Operations Manager, Keswick Ministries
PO Box 6, Keswick, Cumbria, CA12 4GJ

email:
Website: www.keswickministries.org

**Other books
from Keswick Ministries**

Faith in the Face of Danger: Nehemiah
by Jonathan Lamb

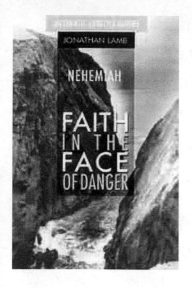

How do we hold onto our faith when we face difficulties and dangers? How do we maintain our integrity in a world which increasingly pressurises us to abandon it? What should our priorities be? How do we build a community that will show the love of God to those who don't know him yet? These are not new questions, and Nehemiah faced them a long, long time ago.

Based on studies in Nehemiah given by Jonathan Lamb at the Keswick Convention.
Additional material includes questions, discussion points, review sections and further study.
Suitable for individual or group use

'Crisp, clear and challenging. Interlaced with humour and arresting anecdote … a stimulating book for both individual and group study.'
Vinoth Ramachandra, IFES

'Nehemiah showed courageous faith at a crucial hour in the nation; the original Bible teaching of this book came in a crucial year for the Keswick Convention; its content should nerve every Christian for testing days ahead.'
Philip H. Hacking, former Chairman of the Keswick Convention

'Jonathan Lamb, at his heart-warming, challenging best. Life-changing stuff.'
Richard Cunningham, UCCF Student Ministries

'The message of Nehemiah – so relevant for today's church – is explained and applied with great skill.'
Ian Coffey, Mutley Baptist Church

ISBN: 1-85078-580-5
Available from your local Christian bookshop or www.WesleyOwen.com

Connect with the Heart of God
by Charles Price and Elizabeth McQuoid

Charles Price's commentary digs deep into the letter to the Hebrews and opens up the world of these first-century believers to us, helping to bridge the gap between the world of the Bible and our own.

Hebrews was written to address some of the fundamental misunderstandings about Jesus that the Jewish people had. The author is writing to correct their ignorance of who Christ was and to explain how Jesus Christ completes and fulfils Israel's history, Israel's law, Israel's ceremonial rituals and Israel's priesthood. This is a readable and incisive look at an essential book of the New Testament.

Additional material includes questions, discussion points, ideas for actions and further study.
Suitable for individual or group use.

'A practical and heart-warming introduction to Hebrews' profoundly encouraging message.'
Jonathan Lamb, Langham Partnership International

Charles Price is the Senior Pastor of The Peoples Church in Toronto, Canada. Prior to this he worked as Principal of Capernwray Bible School. He has preached in many parts of the world and has often written on discipleship and the Bible.

Elizabeth McQuoid earned her Master of Divinity in America. She writes for a number of Christian publications.

ISBN: 1-85078-579-1
Available from your local Christian bookshop or www.WesleyOwen.com

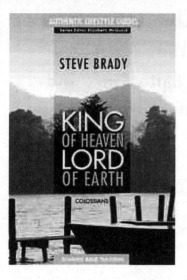

King of Heaven, Lord of Earth: Colossians

by Steve Brady and Elizabeth McQuoid

'Therefore, as God's chosen people, holy and dearly loved, clothe yourselves with compassion, kindness, humility, gentleness and patience.' Colossians 3:12

Keswick speaker Steve Brady examines the book of Colossians, one of Paul's most readable letters. Written with his trademark searching insight and humour, it will unlock the book of Colossians in all its glory. Topics covered include growing in Christian maturity, how to keep away from deceptive teaching, living out God's standards in the community and the sufficiency of Christ.

Additional material includes questions, discussion points, ideas for actions and further study.
Suitable for individual or group use.

'A book that unwraps the message of Colossians and places it slap bang in the middle of our twenty-first century world.'
Ian Coffey, Mutley Baptist Church, Plymouth

'Few people are able to communicate theological truth in a way that "grounds" it into our everyday life, as Steve Brady. I enthusiastically commend it.'
John Glass, Elim

'Biblical, lively, practical, creative … a terrific resource.'
Alistair Begg, Parkside Church, USA

Steve Brady studied at London Bible College, before serving in Baptist and Free Evangelical pastorates in Buckinghamshire, Leicester, East London and Bournemouth. He is currently the Principal of Moorlands College.

Elizabeth McQuoid earned her Master of Divinity in America. She writes for several Christian publications.

ISBN: 1-85078-481-7

Available from your local Christian bookshop or www.WesleyOwen.com

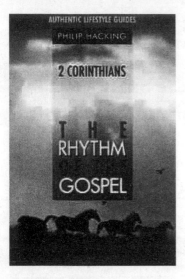

Rhythm of the Gospel
by Philip Hacking and

Elizabeth McQuoid

Strength through weakness, power through frailty, life through death, blessing through sacrifice, and glory through suffering – this is the Rhythm of the Gospel of 2 Corinthians 2–7.

Philip Hacking takes a detailed look at these verses and challenges us not just to believe and accept the gospel but to live it out. This means living lives that present the urgency and compassion of the gospel, preaching messages that preserve its integrity, and persevering though hardships because of the hope it contains. As we read, Paul opens his heart and he shares the loneliness of ministry. But he also reveals the key to being focused. To know what spurred Paul on, what made him joyful in the darkest days, you need to study these chapters. This is God speaking across the centuries, inviting you to share the timeless gospel message.

This study guide aims to take God's word and bring it alive. It provides you with a commentary on the text and questions to help you understand and apply what you've learnt.

Additional material includes questions, discussion points, ideas for actions and further study.

Suitable for individual or group use.

'Fresh, lively and instructive – what more could you ask for?'

Stephen Gaukroger, Senior Pastor, Goldhill Baptist Church

Philip Hacking was formerly Minister at Christ Church, Fulwood, Sheffield. He has been part of the Keswick Convention for over forty years and has written several books.

Elizabeth McQuoid earned her Master of Divinity in America. She writes for several Christian publications.

ISBN: 1-85078-573-2

Available from your local Christian bookshop or www.WesleyOwen.com